BRITAIN IN OLD PHOTOGRAPHS

EAST LANCASHIRE AT WAR

N I C K   D U N N A C H I E

SUTTON PUBLISHING LIMITED

Sutton Publishing Limited
Phoenix Mill · Thrupp · Stroud
Gloucestershire · GL5 2BU

First published 1995

Reprinted in 2002

British Library Cataloguing in Publication Data.
A catalogue record for this book is available from
the British Library.

ISBN 0-7509-1074-7

Typeset in 9/10 Sabon.
Typesetting and origination by
Sutton Publishing Limited.
Printed in Great Britain by
J.H. Haynes & Co. Ltd, Sparkford.

> To those who understood what freedom meant and
> laboured to protect it

Contents

WOMEN'S AUXILIARY
TERRITORIAL SERVICE

MECHANISED TRANSPORT
TRAINING CORPS

ENTERTAINMENTS
NATIONAL SERVICE
ASSOCIATION

FIRST AID NURSING
YEOMANRY

WOMEN'S AUXILIARY
AIR FORCE

AIR RAID PRECAUTIONS

NAVY, ARMY, & AIR
FORCE INSTITUTES

ROYAL NAVAL
PATROL SERVICE

WAR ORGANISATION OF
BRITISH RED CROSS SOCIETY
& ORDER OF   St.JOHN

WOMEN'S LAND ARMY

METROPOLITAN POLICE
WAR RESERVE

METROPOLITAN
SPECIAL CONSTABULARY

CIVIL NURSING RESERVE

AUXILIARY
FIRE SERVICE

VOLUNTARY WORKERS
FOR THE FORCES

MERCHANT NAVY

NATIONAL AIR
RAID PRECAUTIONS
ANIMALS COMMITTEE

WOMEN'S VOLUNTARY
SERVICES

THE FRENCH
OF GREAT BRITAIN

WOMEN'S ROYAL
NAVAL SERVICE
(P.O. Badge)

Badges of the Auxiliary Services. Most of these badges need no description. The Mechanized Transport Training Corps was a voluntary organization of women transport drivers, etc. The RN Patrol Service had a minesweeping and an anti-submarine branch; the shark with its death-wound represents a U-boat. The ARP badge gave place to one with the initials CD (Civil Defence), and when the fire service was nationalized its badge bore the letter NFS. Later, too, a shoulder flash superseded the Home Guard armlet.

Introduction

In the 1930s the growing military might and aspirations of the German nation had indicated that Europe might once again be embroiled in a conflict that would draw in the nations of the world, less than 20 years after the Great War. A few people, most notably Winston Churchill, gave voice to their thoughts; their fears materialised when Germany, which had already annexed Austria and several parts of Czechoslovakia, invaded Poland. France and Great Britain, having already stated that they would defend Poland, requested that the German troops be removed. The request was ignored and France and Great Britain declared war against the Germans on 3 September 1939. A Rawtenstall man, James Melia, a veteran of the Great War, who in his time in the trenches had been wounded three times and buried alive on one occasion, recorded the declaration in his diary: 'All the country was waiting and wondering what was going to happen, then it was announced on the radio that the Prime Minister was to speak to the nation. He did, and told us we were at war with Germany. Sall Parkinson who, with her brother Howarth Parkinson, was in our house, exclaimed, "My God, what is going to happen to us all?" I answered that thousands of people listening now would not be alive to listen to the announcement that the war with Germany was over; that will be in about four years time if we were to be victorious, if less than four, we would have lost.'

King George VI also spoke to the nation that day:

> For the second time in the lives of most of us we are at war. We have been forced into a conflict. For we are called, with our allies, to meet the challenge of a principle, which, if it were to prevail, would be fatal to any civilised order in the world. It is the principle which permits a State, in the selfish pursuit of power, to disregard its treaties and its solemn pledges; which sanctions the use of force, or threat of force, against the sovereignty and independence of other States. There may be dark days ahead, and war can be no longer confined to the battlefield. But we can only do the right as we see the right, and reverently commit our cause to God. May He bless and keep us all.

The knowledge that a new war would not be confined to the battlefield had already been taken to heart, for before September 1939 protective measures had been taking place. As early as 1937 Members of Parliament had voted for the erection of air raid shelters in many towns and cities; air raid precautions had been introduced; plans had been made for the evacuation of major towns and cities; military training had been made compulsory for men of the age group 20–21; a general call had been made for people to volunteer for the National Services; plans for food rationing had been made; and increases had been made in the budgets for the production of munitions and aircraft.

At the end of August, the situation was so grave that evacuation plans were put into operation and on the night of 2 September full black-out conditions were enforced.

The actual outbreak of war saw considerable changes in the towns of East Lancashire, with the implementation of many of the plans which had been laid out. Food Committees were set up and people were called upon to carry gas-masks at all times; those who didn't were reminded to do so by air raid wardens and police officers.

There were signs of military activity with the khaki-clad Territorials and Reservists setting off to join their units, whilst policemen carried not only their gas masks but also steel helmets.

Many buildings were sand-bagged, and air raid shelters and control centres were manned twenty-four hours a day, whilst factory hooters and sirens were silenced, only to be sounded again in the event of an impending air raid. Signs were erected indicating the way to the nearest ARP shelter, trench, or First Aid Post. The great fear of such attacks caused places of public entertainment such as cinemas to be closed, although they were allowed to reopen the week after, but with a curfew of 10 p.m. So great was the fear of aerial bombardment that the government had expected 100,000 casualties during the first few weeks of the war; hospitals had been cleared, mortuaries stacked with cardboard coffins and lime-pits dug to cope with the dead. This estimate may have been based on the statistics gleaned from the First World War, when for every ton of bombs dropped in civilian areas there were ten casualties. One Public Information leaflet advised people to carry a luggage label bearing their name and address.

Reduced services were provided on both bus and railway systems, and the night-time black-out meant that motor vehicles made their way slowly through the dark with covered headlights and whitened wings, and only yellow lines down the centre of the roads and white lines at the kerbs to guide them.

The need for permanent black-outs led to a rush on the shops for suitable material and stocks occasionally ran out. People were seen putting up their coverings, coming outside to check, and then going inside again to readjust their work. Shopkeepers themselves had difficulty in ensuring their windows were properly covered, and many had light traps installed on their doors to ensure no light escaped on the entrance of a customer.

On Saturday 29 September the National Registration of every person in the country commenced, in preparation for the issuing of identity cards and ration books. The latter were distributed in November and the first food rationing was implemented on 8 January. It is doubtful that anyone at the time could have imagined that some foodstuffs would be rationed until 1954.

The government exhorted the general public to play their part in the war effort; posters urged people to grow food in their gardens or in allotments, save money and buy War Bonds, not to travel, not to waste food, and neither to spread rumours nor listen to them.

Despite all the Government's efforts, a growing lack of confidence in the way the war was being waged led to the downfall of Chamberlain, and Winston Churchill took over the premiership in May 1940. His first speech to the nation set the tone for many future discourses which were to rally the citizens and unite the country:

After this battle in France abates its force there will come a battle for this island, for all that Britain is and all that Britain means. That will be the struggle. In that supreme emergency we shall not hesitate to take every step, even the most drastic, to call forth from our people the last ounce of effort of which they are capable. The interests of property and the hours of labour are nothing compared with the struggle for life and honour and freedom to which we have vowed ourselves. Today is Trinity Sunday. Centuries ago words were written to be a call and a spur to faithful servants of truth and justice: 'Arm yourselves, and be ye men of valour, and be in readiness for the conflict, for it is better for us to perish in battle than to look on the outrage of our nation and our altars. As the will of God is in Heaven, even so let Him do.'

This call on God was supplemented by the passing of the Emergency Powers (Defence) Act on 22 May 1940, which in effect gave the Government the power to take complete control of all persons and property in the country.

After the fall of France in June 1940, Britain was the only country in Europe to continue the fight against Germany, and the world in general expected her to fall at any moment. Around the end of July 1940 a German propaganda leaflet, dropped by the Luftwaffe, and picked up in Helmshore, Rossendale, fairly accurately stated the respective conditions of Britain and Germany:

On July 19, the Fuhrer and Chancellor Adolf Hitler addressed the German Reichstag with a speech in which he gave the German nation an account of the military operations carried out up to the present. The Fuhrer described the German Army's wonderful achievements in Norway and on the Western Front, which in every case led to the complete rout of the enemy within a few weeks. He then dealt generally with Germany's position after ten months of the war, and stated that it was singularly favourable in view of the coming final battle with England. The German people, he said, were united as never before in their history, and would follow their leaders to the end. As far as food supplies were concerned, the war could last for any length of time. Since wide areas in Europe had by now been occupied, Germany would be able to draw on inexhaustible resources of raw materials. From now on, time would work for Germany. Germany commanded the strongest forces the world had ever seen, and was firmly resolved, side by side with allied Italy, to throw them into an attack against Britain, if this should prove necessary. In spite of

Germany's overwhelming superiority and her unique strategic advantages – as opposed to the utter isolation of Britain – the Fuhrer once more upheld the policy of an understanding with Britain, which he has followed all these years, and again appealed to reason and common sense before starting out on a battle which, in its consequences for England, is beyond imagination.

Despite the odds, with no talk of capitulation, and no thought of defeat, Britain fought on alone until Hitler broke his pact with Stalin and invaded Russia on 30 June 1941. However, it was not until America's entry into the war (two and a quarter years too late, and forced on them by Japan, according to many contemporary British accounts), that any hope of victory could be sustained.

The six years it took to help defeat Germany and Japan cost Britain dearly; over a quarter of a million members of the armed forces were killed and more than ninety thousand civilians; financially the cost was at least £30,000,000,000, and the country was brought to the brink of bankruptcy.

It is against this background that we look at the experiences of those who lived in East Lancashire during the dark days of total conflict. Of course, the war here was very different from that of Manchester, Liverpool, Coventry, the Midlands, London and the southern counties, in that only minor air raids took place, and few bombs were dropped. However, as was the case with the rest of the country, many local families had relatives risking their lives in the Armed Forces, and telegrams notifying them of the death or capture of a loved one were as common here as elsewhere. In Lancashire, too, all the inconveniences of war were endured but, like the rest of the nation, Lancastrians looked to Europe, didn't like what they saw, and with great moral and physical courage, set about rectifying the situation. Long working hours, voluntary service, rationing, petty restrictions, total control by the government, high taxation, the risk of death, all were endured in order to gain the final victory.

Their industry, bravery and sacrifice ought to be remembered, not only so that all due honour can be paid, but also so that their standards can be used as benchmarks by future generations.

RATIONING

For most people, the mention of rationing initially brings to mind the rationing of food, and although this was of great importance, it ought to be remembered that a wide variety of goods either went 'on the ration', or came to be in very short supply. Many mills and factories were switched from the production of peacetime articles to weapons, munitions and uniforms.

Food, however, was the first to be rationed, and how this was to be managed was explained in a publication issued in July 1939, called *Your Food in War-time*. This pointed out that a large amount of our foodstuffs came from overseas by ships on trade routes which were vulnerable in times of war, and that the government had already stockpiled certain food in addition to the amounts needed for normal commercial requirements. Individuals were requested, if they could afford it, to stock up on certain items, such as meat and fish in cans or glass jars, flour, suet, canned or dried milk, sugar, tea, cocoa and plain biscuits.

Concerning Central Control, it declared: 'Should war come, the Government would take over responsibility for obtaining the main food supplies for the country, and for distributing them through all the stages down to the consumer. This would ensure that every precaution could be taken against war time risks. The price of food would be controlled and supplies directed wherever they were needed.

For this purpose, the existing organization of the food trades would be used so far as possible, and all food traders – importers, manufacturers, wholesalers and retailers – would work under the direction of a Ministry of Food. The Ministry would act for the benefit of the country as a whole and be assisted by representatives of the various trades. As far as local distribution was concerned:

In each area food control would be in the hands of a local committee, which would be set up at the outbreak of war. The membership of these committees would be chosen to represent the general body of consumers in the area. The principal duty of these local Food Control Committees would be to look after the interests of the consumers. Shopkeepers would be licensed to trade by these committees. Maximum prices would be fixed by the Ministry for each controlled food, and would be shown clearly in the shop windows.

Regarding the population itself the leaflet stated: 'rationing will be applied to five foodstuffs – butcher's meat, bacon and ham, sugar, butter and margarine, and cooking fats,' with the ominous addition that 'later it might be necessary to add other articles.' By March 1940 the produce rationed included butter, 4 oz; sugar, 12 oz; bacon or ham uncooked, and meat to the value of 1s. 2d. More foodstuffs were rationed as time went by, including tea and milk. To save space on cargo ships, dried egg powder, dried vegetables and boned meat were introduced. Occasionally extra rations were granted, though at other times the ration of certain produce such as milk was increased and decreased. Bread, in the form of Victory loaves, was made from homegrown wheat, which used a large part of the husk and as a result looked grey. Surprisingly, bread was not rationed until after the war.

There was, of course, the black market where produce, either on or off the ration, could be purchased but at a much higher price. Although the black market tended to occur in cities and larger towns, there was a certain amount of trading taking place in East Lancashire. For instance, it has been commonly stated that bananas were unavailable during the war. 'Not if you'd got cigarettes,' recalls a certain wartime tobacconist from Padiham. A licence to slaughter had to be obtained by farmers who wanted to butcher a beast, but a farmer's daughter remembers that 'every farm had a spare pig'. One farmer in Whitworth was visited by an inspector from the Food Ministry when a pig was to be slaughtered. The farmer showed one half of the pig to the inspector who then asked, 'Where's the other half?' 'That shed over there,' said the farmer. They went into the shed to have a look at the other half, and came out, much to the relief of the farmer, without the inspector noticing that each half of the pig had a tail. In Clitheroe, Bryn Joynson remembers several methods by which members of the Royal Engineers who were stationed there during the war augmented their pay. Explosives were used in exercises in the River Ribble, and the dead and stunned fish were sold by the sappers to the local populace at 1s. a pound. The sappers also tested anti-personnel mines. The trick here was to set the mine, scatter a little corn around it, then wait until a flock of pigeons arrived, and then explode the mine. 9d. a pigeon was the goin0g rate.

Your Food in War-time, published in July 1939, gave the population of Great Britain an indication of what would happen to their food supplies in the event of war. Before rationing began, application forms were sent to every householder, who had to give particulars of everyone living in his home. These forms were returned to the local food office set up by the local Food Control Committee, which issued the ration books, one for each person. Everyone then registered at a retail shop of their own choice for each rationed food.

For children under six years of age, there was a child's ration book, the difference being that a child was allowed half the amount of butcher's meat allowed for an adult. On the other hand, the allowance for a worker with a strenuous job gave him a larger quantity of meat. For catering and other institutions, special arrangements were to be made.

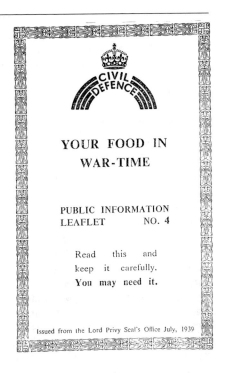

CIVIL DEFENCE

YOUR FOOD IN WAR-TIME

PUBLIC INFORMATION LEAFLET   NO. 4

Read   this   and
keep   it   carefully.
You   may   need   it.

Issued from the Lord Privy Seal's Office July, 1939

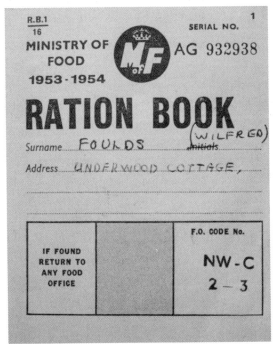

R.B.1 / 16

MINISTRY OF FOOD
1953-1954

SERIAL NO.   1

AG 932938

RATION BOOK

Surname FOULDS   (WILFRED) Initials

Address UNDERWOOD COTTAGE,

IF FOUND RETURN TO ANY FOOD OFFICE		F.O. CODE No.
		NW-C 2-3

The ration books contained coupons, a certain number for each week. The Ministry decided how much food each coupon represented, and the owner of the book was entitled to buy that amount. In the case of meat, the amount was expressed in money, thus giving a choice between a larger amount of a cheaper cut, or a smaller amount of a more expensive cut. In the case of other foods, the amount was by weight.

This ration book was for the year 1953–4. Few people would have guessed that rationing would have gone on for so long. In Britain, meat was the last product to be de-rationed in 1954.

A few samples of the many thousands of posters which were put out by the government.

Close-up of the sign outside the
British Restaurant, Mayson Street,
Blackburn.

Outside the British Restaurant,
Mayson Street, Blackburn, February
1942. Early in the war, the
government began to establish
British Restaurants, which provided
a reasonable meal without requiring
the use of a ration card. By 1943 the
number of these had risen to over
2,000 and was rapidly increasing.
The number of meals served in these
restaurants, as well as works
canteens, catering establishments,
etc., was 180 million a week.

Two interior views of the British Restaurant in Mayson Street, Blackburn.

WHAT YOUR CLOTHING COUPONS CAN BUY

WOMEN AND GIRLS

	Women	Girls
Unlined macintosh or cape...	9	7
Other macintoshes, capes, raincoats, coats (over 28in. long)	14	11
Jacket, blazer, short coat ...	11	8
Dress, gown, frock (woollen)	11	8
Dress, gown, frock (other)...	7	5
Gym. tunic, girls' skirt with bodice	8	6
Blouse, jumper, shawl, bed jacket	5	3
Skirt	7	5
Apron, pinafore	3	2
Pyjamas	8	6
Nightdress	6	5
Petticoat, slip, combinations, cami-knickers, bathing costume	4	3
Other undergarments	3	2
Pair of stockings	2	1
Pair of socks	1	1
Two handkerchiefs	1	1
Scarf, gloves	2	2
Pair slippers, boots, leggings, gaiters	3	2

MEN AND BOYS

	Men	Boys
Unlined macintosh or cape...	9	7
Other macintoshes, capes, raincoats, overcoats	16	11
Coat, jacket, blazer	13	8
Waistcoat, pullover	5	3
Trousers	8	6
Corduroy trousers	5	5
Shorts	5	3
Overalls, dungarees	6	4
Dressing gowns, bathing gowns	8	6
Nightshirt or pyjamas	8	6
Shirt (woollen)	8	6
Shirt (other)	5	4
Undergarments, bathing costume, child's blouse	4	2
Socks, stockings, bathing trunks	3	1
Collar, tie, cuffs	1	1
Two handkerchiefs	1	1
Scarf, gloves	2	2
Pair boots, shoes	7	3

CLOTH WIDTH

	Wool per yard	Other Cloths per yard
Not over 3in.	Exempt	Exempt
Over 3in. and not over 9in.	½	¼
Over 9in. and not over 15in.	1	⅔
Over 15in. and not over 21in.	1½	1
Over 21in. and not over 27in.	2	1½
Over 27in. and not over 33in.	2½	1¾
Over 33in. and not over 39in.	3	2
Over 39in. and not over 45in.	3½	2¼
Over 45in. and not over 51in.	4	2¾
Over 51in. and not over 57in.	4½	3

HAND KNITTING WOOL

One coupon for each 2 ozs.

Articles not rationed are:—

Children's clothing up to age four.
Boiler suits, bib and brace overalls.
Hats, caps, clogs.
Sewing thread, elastic.
Mending wool and silk.
Boot and shoe laces.
Tapes, braids, ribbon up to 3in. wide.
Lace and lace net.
Sanitary towels.
Braces, suspenders, garters.
Hand haberdashery.
Black-out cloth dyed black.
All second-hand articles.

KEEP THIS TABLE FOR REFERENCE

'What your Clothing Coupons can buy', June 1941.

1942-43 CLOTHING BOOK

This book may not be used until the holder's name, full postal address and National Registration (Identity Card) Number have been plainly written below IN INK.

NAME_____*L. H. GRAYSHAN*_____
(BLOCK LETTERS)

ADDRESS_____*40 GRANGE ROAD*_____
(BLOCK LETTERS)

(TOWN)_____*RAWTENSTALL*_____(COUNTY)_____*LANCS.*

NATIONAL REGISTRATION (IDENTITY CARD) NUMBER

NWXR / 25 / 1   N. R.

Read the instructions within carefully, and take great care not to lose this book

Page 1

A clothing book for 1942–3. Clothing was rationed for the first time on 2 June 1941, but to prevent forestalling, the extra margarine coupons in the food ration book were to be used until a new ration book was issued.

On 3 February 1942 a list of maximum clothes prices was laid down, and it was decreed that a man's suit must cost no more than £4 18s. 8d.

3 March 1942 saw some headlines which read 'Hemlines set to rise.' The Board of Trade announced a new utility cloth and restricted the number of styles people could have to get rid of all unnecessary frills. For instance, men could not have double-breasted coats or sleeve buttons, and there were to be no turn-ups on trousers. However, utility suits made by authorized tailors were made to a standard price.

Women's fashions included 'bare legs for patriotism' in May 1942, and in January 1943 it was demanded that only standard grey or blue school uniforms be allowed in order to save on dye.

According to a Board of Trade survey, it was announced on 17 May 1942 that clothes rationing had saved the country £600 million and 500,000 tons of shipping, while releasing thousands of workers for war factories.

On 1 February 1944 clothing restrictions were lifted, and men could look forward to turn-ups, lined pockets and double breasted jackets. Twenty-six coupons were required for non-austerity suits, and twenty-four for suits made with utility cloth. In addition, women could look forward to pleats and plenty of buttons, but by September 1947 they were being asked to avoid the trend for longer skirts and save cloth in the national interest.

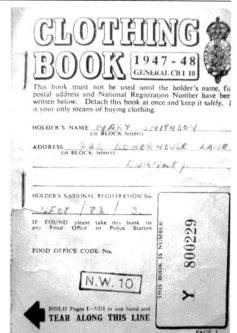

Clothing ration book cover and interior,
1947–8.

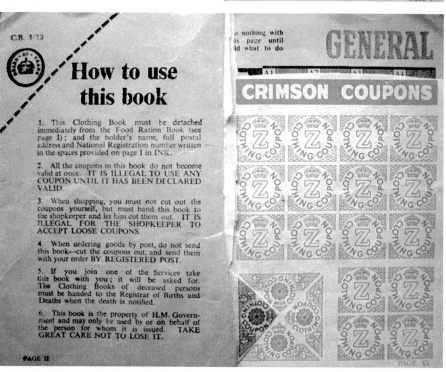

The health of the nation was important to the government and it used both posters and lectures to prevent a variety of illnesses and diseases from spreading.

The fair distribution of the available food helped to increase the overall health of the nation. Rationing ensured everybody had an adequate diet, and subsidies for a wide range of produce kept the prices affordable for everybody.

This 'We want your kitchen waste' poster was a reminder that everything had a value to the war effort, even the most basic of items. In March 1942 civil servants' pencil sharpeners were withdrawn to save pencils.

Section Two

AIR RAID PRECAUTIONS

Well before the outbreak of war, booklets dealing with the possibility of air raids were being published. The Home Office first published two Air Raid Precautions Handbooks in 1936, No. 1 being subtitled *Personal Protection Against Gas*, and No. 2 *Anti-Gas Precautions and First Aid for Air Raid Casualties*. In 1938 every household received a copy of *The Protection Of Your Home Against Air Raids*, published by the Home Office. In the introduction, Samuel Hoare states:

> If this country were ever at war the target of the enemy's bombers would be the staunchness of the people at home. We all hope and work to prevent war but, while there is risk of it, we cannot afford to neglect the duty of preparing ourselves and the country for such an emergency. This book is being sent out to help each householder to realise what he can do, if the need arises, to make his home and his household more safe against air attack. If the emergency comes the country will look for her safety not only to her sailors and soldiers and airmen, but also to the organized courage and foresight of every household.

The booklet was concerned mainly with creating a refuge-room in the home, and what equipment and stores would be useful for it, what to do in an air raid, and some brief advice about the use of gas masks which the government would soon be issuing to the general public. Although the Geneva Gas Protocol of 1925 had banned the use of poison gas between the warring nations, little trust was given to the enemy on that issue. In consequence, a great deal of time and expense was expended upon ensuring that everyone in the country knew what to do to protect themselves and their families from gas attacks. As early as 1939 it had already been made compulsory for schoolchildren to practise gas mask drill.

Local air raid precaution organizations had already been set up and air raid wardens appointed, and householders were advised to get further information from them as how to best go about protecting their families and homes.

In January 1939 a more detailed booklet was published, *A Concise, Fully Illustrated and Practical Guide for the Householder and Air-Raid Warden*. It explained the three methods which an enemy, operating from a distance with high-powered, fast bombing aeroplanes, might use to terrorize the civilian population and disorganize the national services:

1. High Explosive Attacks, involving the use of highly destructive bombs to cause destruction, injury and loss of life.
2. Incendiary Attacks, i.e. the use of fire bombs to cause widespread fires so as to create panic and disorganize essential services, especially the ARP Organization.
3. Gas Attacks, involving the release, from bombs or as spray, of dangerous liquid gases, vapour gases, or poisonous smokes, intended to injure or incapacitate the public, to nullify or hamper precautions taken against (1) and (2), and to make difficult the work of rescue and first aid.

There was also the suggestion that enemy aeroplanes flying at low altitudes might use machine guns to attack crowds of civilians or masses of soldiers, and that during an air attack death or injury may also be caused by falling shrapnel and bullets from our own anti-aircraft guns.

The *Air Raid Precautions Training Manual No. 1*, published in 1940, describes the general organization of Civil Defence, the purpose of which was to minimize the damage caused by any enemy aircraft that managed to penetrate the active defences. Civil Defence was the responsibility of local authorities in the United Kingdom, working under the general direction of the Ministry of Home Security.

A national warning system had been set up which sent messages to any area which was considered to be due for an attack. In these areas an 'Action Warning' lasting two minutes was sounded on variable pitch sirens or a succession of five second blasts on a fixed pitch hooter.

Whether a raid actually took place or not, members of the various branches of the Civil Defence were prepared for any eventuality. Amongst the Air Raid wardens' duties was the assessment of damage, reporting it and guiding the ARP services sent to deal with it. The Auxiliary Fire Service was to assist the local fire brigade if there was too much for them to cope with. Specially trained chemists formed the Gas Identification Service, and Decontamination Squads were ready to deal with gas attacks. First Aid Parties, Posts and Hospitals were ready for the injured. Rescue parties were available to help trapped people, and the buildings they had been trapped in would be dealt with by the Demolition and Repair services. Unexploded bombs, shells and crashed aircraft were also attended to by specialists.

LANCASHIRE CONSTABULARY.

IMPORTANT NOTICE

AIR RAID PRECAUTIONS

BLACK-OUT

Night of 15/16th May, 1939.

In connection with the Home Defence Exercises, it is intended to "Black-out" the whole of Lancashire for a short period during the night of 15/16th May, and the Secretary of State has asked all Districts to co-operate by putting out all lights that may be visible from the air on the night of 15/16th May, 1939, between the hours of 12-30 a.m. and 2-0 a.m.

HOW HOUSEHOLDERS CAN HELP.

HOUSEHOLDERS AND ALL OTHER OCCUPIERS OF PREMISES ARE ACCORDINGLY ASKED TO ASSIST BY ENSURING THAT LIGHTS IN THEIR PREMISES ARE EXTINGUISHED OR SCREENED BY DARK CURTAINS OR BLINDS, BETWEEN 12-30 A.M. AND 2-0 A.M. IN THE EARLY MORNING OF 16TH MAY. IT IS PARTICULARLY DESIRABLE THAT EXTERNAL LIGHTS AND OTHER LIGHTS DIRECTLY VISIBLE FROM THE SKY SHOULD BE EXTINGUISHED OR SCREENED.

STREET LIGHTING WILL BE RESTRICTED.

As lighting in streets will be restricted, vehicles should, so far as possible, keep off the roads during the darkened period.

It is emphasised that there is no intention, in connection with the "Black-out," of cutting off lighting or power supplies at the mains.

Preston, May 1939.

A. F. HORDERN,
Chief Constable of Lancashire.

SEPTIMUS WARD LTD., Manchester Road Printing Works, PRESTON.

Civil Defence armband.

SERIAL No. 13558

Lancashire County Council
A.R.P. SERVICES

The Bearer

M ___Patricia Windle___

is a member of the A.R.P. Service and should be afforded all possible facilities to pass to his/her duty.

Geo Eckerlin.

Clerk of the Lancashire County Council.

LOCAL
AUTHORITY **HASLINGDEN.**

HOLDER'S
SIGNATURE ___Patricia Windle___

N.R. No. | NUYJ | 92 | 3
[SEE BACK]

ARP Card belonging to Pat Fisher, née Windle. Pat worked for the Civil Defence at Haslingden with the ARP, and remembers that when they had to sound the alarm there was always a fight to see who could get to press the button first.

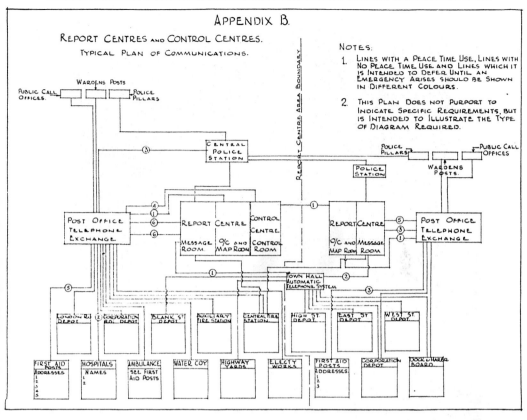

APPENDIX B.

REPORT CENTRES AND CONTROL CENTRES.

TYPICAL PLAN OF COMMUNICATIONS.

NOTES:

1. LINES WITH A PEACE TIME USE, LINES WITH NO PEACE TIME USE AND LINES WHICH IT IS INTENDED TO DEFER UNTIL AN EMERGENCY ARISES SHOULD BE SHOWN IN DIFFERENT COLOURS.

2. THIS PLAN DOES NOT PURPORT TO INDICATE SPECIFIC REQUIREMENTS, BUT IS INTENDED TO ILLUSTRATE THE TYPE OF DIAGRAM REQUIRED.

This diagram is taken from *Local Communications and Reporting of Air Raid Damage*, first published in April 1939, and issued by the Home Office (Air Raid Precautions Department). The illustration shows a typical plan of the communications which would be required for the Report Centres and Control Centres to deal with emergencies. This is taken from the second edition, which was published in September 1939.

All the ARP services were operated and controlled by local headquarters established in Report and Control Centres. Fortunately for East Lancashire, although all the usual preparations had been made, there were very few bombs dropped in the area.

GAS ATTACK

HOW TO PUT ON YOUR GAS MASK

Always keep your gas mask with you —day and night. Learn to put it on quickly. Practise wearing it.

1. Hold your breath. 2. Hold mask in front of face, with thumbs inside straps.
3. Thrust chin well forward into mask, pull straps over head as far as they will go.
4. Run finger round face-piece taking care head-straps are not twisted.

IF THE GAS RATTLES SOUND

1. Hold your breath. Put on mask wherever you are. Close window.

2. If out of doors, take off hat, put on your mask. Turn up collar.

3. Put on gloves or keep hands in pockets. Take cover in nearest building.

IF YOU GET GASSED

BY VAPOUR GAS Keep your gas mask on even if you feel discomfort
If discomfort continues go to First Aid Post

BY LIQUID or BLISTER GAS

1 Dab, but *don't rub* the splash with handkerchief. Then destroy handkerchief.

2 Rub No. 2 Ointment well into place.
(Buy a 6d. jar now from any chemist).
In emergency chemists supply Bleach Cream free.

3 If you can't get Ointment or Cream within 5 minutes wash place with soap and warm water.

4 Take off at once any garment splashed with gas.

PRINTED FOR H.M. STATIONERY OFFICE BY FOSH & CROSS LTD., LONDON. (S1/5041)

Hitler will send no warning – so always carry your gas mask

The threat of gas attacks both before and during the early part of the war, despite Germany being a signatory to the Geneva Convention banning the use of gas as a weapon, ensured that everyone carried a mask all the time.

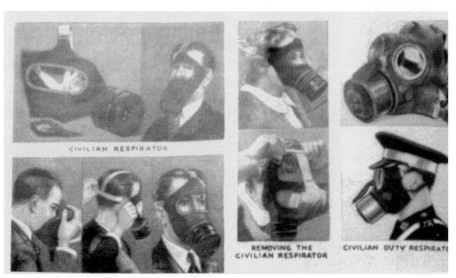

Gas masks for ordinary civilians and those performing Civil Defence duties were different.

HOW TO TACKLE A
FIRE BOMB

INDOORS

How a fire-fighting team works:

The team should consist of 3 people.

"Number One" is in charge of the team and operates the pump nozzle.

"Number Two" mans the pump.

"Number Three" fills buckets, relieves "Number Two", watches hose and keeps a general look-out.

1 "Number One" enters the burning room on hands and knees. He opens the door slowly to avoid possible bursts of flame and fumes. He keeps his head back as he opens the door.

2 OUTSIDE the burning room. "Number Two" pumps and "Number Three" brings the water.

3 "Number One" in action. He crawls towards the bomb, head well down, face shielded. He takes whatever cover he can, such as a table or chair.

4 If furniture or hangings are on fire, "Number One" deals with them first, damping them down with the jet. He then turns the spray on to the fire-bomb.

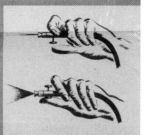

5 How to operate the pump nozzle, showing how to change over quickly from jet to spray.

OUTDOORS

Leave the bomb alone for a short time unless it is likely to set fire to something. Tackle it at once if it falls close to something inflammable

The easiest way to carry a sandbag is to sling it over your shoulder

When approaching the fire-bomb, take care to shield your face with the sandbag.

Don't empty the sandbag on the fire-bomb. Place the sandbag on the bomb.

When you have covered the fire-bomb — do not linger. GET AWAY quickly.

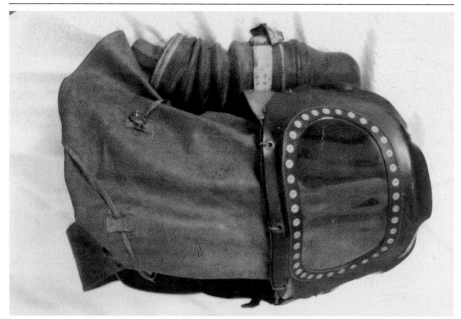

This gas mask, or respirator, was for babies. The child would be placed inside with its head in the upper part with the face mask. The cloth part would be fastened securely around the waist of the baby with the lower part secured by straps between the baby's legs. A hand-pump with a filter attached ensured that the child had a gas-free air supply.

Two methods of dealing with an incendiary bomb. On the left a hoe, scoop and container are being used. On the right the women are using a stirrup hand-pump.

Members of the Auxiliary Fire Service outside the Municipal Offices, Haslingden, not easily recognized because of the sandbags. In the photograph are Ross Warburton, George Cunliffe, Tom Birtwistle, Mr Walsh, Mr Marsden, Tom Flynn and the father of Mrs Elsie Tattersall, the donor of the photograph. In June 1941 the National Fire Service was formed, and the 1,400 local fire brigades in England and Wales were organised into 32 fire forces, while separate arrangements were made for the London region and for Scotland. This sweeping scheme made possible much-needed uniformity in training, equipment and water supply; it also provided for interchange and reinforcement between areas.

In addition to the official Fire Service, many civilians took their turn at firewatching, making sure that if any incendiary bombs landed they were dealt with quickly to prevent further damage. Tom Fisher recalls a time when he worked at the Porritt's mill in Helmshore where there were about a hundred men split into teams of ten, each of which took turns to firewatch at night, making regular patrols of the factory buildings. One of the buildings had been installed with bunks for the occasional use of the firewatchers. However, one section, under the leadership of Billy Fitton, was wakened early one morning by the Fire Brigade who had been called out to a fire on the premises which had destroyed several cars, a lorry and badly damaged a large amount of valuable 3-inch maple timber. The fire had been caused by an electrical fault, but the section leader was never allowed to forget the incident.

Although well away from the centre of Burnley, Towneley Hall, like many buildings, was protected against bombs by sandbags. At Bury Museum an air raid shelter was constructed in the basement, not so much for the protection of the employees, but for the safe-keeping of a landscape painting by Turner.

A Concise, Fully Illustrated and Practical Guide for the Householder and Air-Raid Warden gives a brief explanation of how a high explosive bomb works:

This contains chemicals which, when ignited or detonated (e.g. by explosion of a detonator on impact of the bomb with a hard surface), instantaneously and violently interact to create a great volume of gas. The enormous pressure inside the metal shell causes a most destructive explosion and creates a terrific wind blast all around the point of impact. TNT (Trinitrotoluene), the most powerful explosive yet discovered, expands into about 4,000 times its original volume, and, of course, the heat of the explosion itself causes still further great and rapid expansion of the gases produced.

A direct hit of a 500 lb bomb striking a hard surface would smash up practically everything within a radius of about 50 ft of its point of impact.

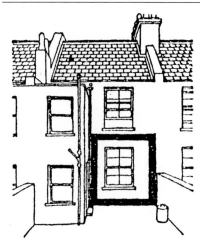

In a two-storeyed terrace house choose a room on the ground floor. The flanking walls will protect you from the blast of a bursting bomb

A cellar or basement is the best position for a refuge-room if it can be made reasonably gas-proof

In a house with only two floors and without a cellar, choose a room on the ground floor so that you have protection overhead

These illustrations from *The Protection of Your Home Against Air Raids* offered advice on the selection of a refuge-room. Another booklet, *A Concise, Fully Illustrated and Practical Guide for the Householder and Air-Raid Warden*, informed its readers:

The force of the exploding bomb could send bits of the metal casing of the bomb flying in all directions, as well as stones, bricks, iron work, pieces of paving. Splinters from a medium size bomb could penetrate a 9-inch brick wall at a distance of 50 feet from the point of impact.

Within 50 feet of a large bomb its wind blast could tear a man to pieces and shatter a brick wall. Further away, the blast could deafen people by bursting their ear drums, or kill them by paralysing their lungs. Windows and doors could be blown in over a wide radius, and the blast so entering could wreck floors and ceilings and cause the sides of the building to collapse.

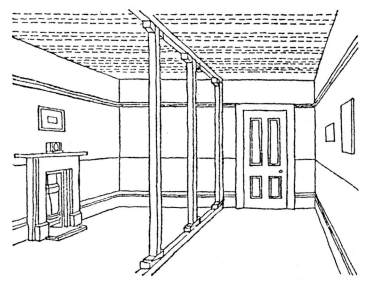

How to support a ceiling

In a refuge-room, additional protection could be gained by using props to support the ceiling in case of a bomb-burst.

The Stirrup hand-pump was specially recommended for dealing with incendiary bombs and the resultant fires. It was supplied with 30 ft of hose and was designed to be used by two or three people. It could either send a jet of water about 30 ft, or a spray of water about 15 ft. Spraying the incendiary bomb with water increased the activity of the burning bomb by supplying it with more oxygen, which would help the bomb to burn out more quickly. The advantages of the hand-pump were that it enabled the fire to be fought from a safe distance, and away from the intense heat and smoke, as well as providing a means of attacking both the fire and the bomb, each of which required separate treatment. It was economical with water, 6 to 8 gallons being sufficient to extinguish the bomb and any normal fire in a room in about five minutes.

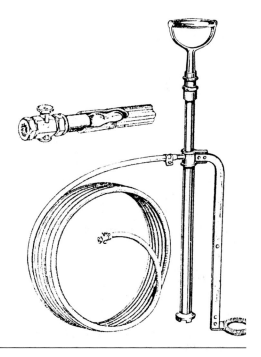

The Morrison 'Table' Shelter was for use in the refuge-room. In quiet periods it could be used as a table, as shown, or as a bed. In the event of an air raid, the side panels at the far end of the table would be attached by the householder. The assembly instructions state:

The walls of most houses give good shelter from blast and splinters from a bomb falling nearby. The bomb, however, may also bring down part of the house, and additional protection from the fall of walls, floors and ceilings is therefore very essential. This is what the indoor shelter has been designed to give.

You may have to put the shelter into the room where you need a table; but if you have a choice, choose the room whose walls give you the best protection. Protection is needed especially up to the level of the top of the shelter (2 ft. 6 ins. high), so the room with the fewest openings down to floor level (doors and French windows) is the best.

A room facing the garden is better than one facing the street, because the soft earth may allow the bomb to go in deep before exploding, thus reducing the danger from bomb splinters. Make a rough plan showing just where the shelter is and in which room, and give it to your Air Raid warden.

The most common type of shelter for the home was the Anderson shelter. This one was installed in the back garden of a house in Holly Avenue, Haslingden, in 1939. In the centre is Joseph Webb, with neighbours Albert Skilling (left), and Arthur Hargreaves (right). The shelter was an object that was exploited by cartoonists. One depicted a small girl standing on top of a shelter, being told by her mother, 'Don't jump up and down, Winnie, you might fall through'.

Interior of the 'Pyramid' air raid shelter made by Foster, Yates & Thom Ltd, Blackburn, photographed in 1940.

Patent 'Pyramid' air raid shelter made by Foster, Yates & Thom Ltd, on display by
Blackpool Tower, 1940.

Reinforcement of Thompson Street surface air raid shelter, Padiham. A large number of surface air raid shelters, with brick walls and concrete roofs, were erected. According to a memorandum regarding the strengthening of surface shelters, it would appear that some of them were so weak that they would collapse if a bomb dropped nearby. The memorandum explained the various ways of reinforcing the shelters to protect against ground-movement and earth-shock caused by a bomb close to the shelter which explodes well below ground; mass splinter attack and blast caused by a nearby bomb which explodes on the surface; and excessive debris-loading. Nothing of course could be done should a bomb score a direct hit.

The entrance of the air raid shelter in the Memorial Park, Padiham.

Construction work being carried out on an underground shelter, adjacent to the cemetery, Padiham. In the photograph are Archie Sullivan, Harry Riley (centre) and George Helm. Harry Riley was a veteran of the First World War, and a tale-teller of some repute.

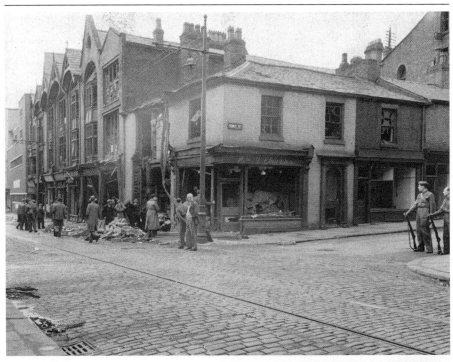

Ainsworth Street bomb damage, August 1940. 'The bomb dropped by a German raider in Ainsworth Street fell at 11.43 pm on 31 August 1940. Its actual weight was never established but the general effect was consistent with the explosion of a bomb of about 200 kilograms weight.' *Northern Daily Telegraph*, 5 September 1945.

Bomb damage at Bennington Street, Blackburn, 30 August 1940.

Tottington.

Taken early in the century, this photograph shows a row of cottages facing St Anne's Church, in Chapel Street, Tottington, near Bury. On 24 December 1944 a V-1 flying bomb was launched from an enemy aircraft and hit the cottages, completely flattening two of the dwellings and badly damaging two others. Seven people were killed outright and another fourteen injured. Two of the dead, James and Teresa Dyson, had entered the village only a few hours before, whilst George Ormerod, an occupant of one of the worst damaged houses, had made a last minute arrangement to spend Christmas in Lyme Regis.

The site of the cottages was later cleared and a memorial garden was planted, in which now rests a plaque bearing the following inscription:

The Whitehead Garden. This was given by Mr and Mrs J.D. Whitehead of Stormer Hill to the people of Tottington to be enjoyed by them for all time in memory of those named below who were killed by a flying bomb on 24th December 1944. Nicholas Conway, Mary Ann Conway, Elizabeth Draper, James Dyson, Teresa Dyson, Ann Greenhalgh, Bertha Greenhalgh.

Bomb damage at the row of cottages in Tottington, December 1944.

A restored Auxiliary Fire Service lorry, in the parade held in Haslingden to commemorate the fiftieth anniversary of VE day.

Five members of the Auxiliary Fire Service, with fire cart, photographed in the grounds of Hillside, Billinge End Lane, Blackburn.

Members of the National Fire Service, Burnley. Third from the right on the front row is Stephen Crabtree.

Chief Officers, Civil Defence Wardens' Service, Burnley, February 1944. Back row, left to right: H. Sutherland, W. Mather, R.C. Rawlinson, H. Hartley, D. Hargreaves, W. Phillips, T. Lawson. Middle row: W. Wearing, W.H. Curson, J. Lancaster, G.H. Todd, P. O'Malia, J. Sutcliffe, J. Knowles, H. Baker, J. Heap. Front row: C. Nadin, H. Thornton, M. Heyworth, J.H. Haffner, W. Green, Insp. R. Smith, K.L. Lovegreen, F.B. Hargreaves, G. Rigge, G. Dunkerley.

A group of members of the Civil Defence Group, Burnley.

'J' Group ARP, Burnley, winners of a darts league trophy.

Harry Haffner, George Dunkerley and William Lancaster, Group Wardens and cameramen who made an ARP film in November 1941. It recorded an exercise in which all the elements of Civil Defence participated. The film showed some of the activities in the control centre at Throstle Mill, air raid wardens, fire fighting, the rescue of children from 'bombed out' buildings, and the work of the hospital service in dealing with casualties.

Some members of the Burnley Air Raid Wardens of the Summit Depot, Manchester Road, in civvies.

In some areas in December 1940 there was a shortage of batteries for torches, which the air raid wardens had to supply themselves. This might give some credence to the story of the two wardens who were patrolling together at night with one torch between them. They came to one house, the front door of which could only be approached by a plank stretched over a deep hole dug into the garden. There was a light coming from the front window of the house, so one of the wardens walked across the plank, banged on the door and demanded, very loudly, for the light to be extinguished. The light disappeared and the warden turned to make his way back to the road. However, his colleague had moved on, with the torch, leaving him in total darkness. Much to his chagrin, the warden had to bang on the door and ask for the light to be put on again so that he could negotiate the hazardous route back to the road.

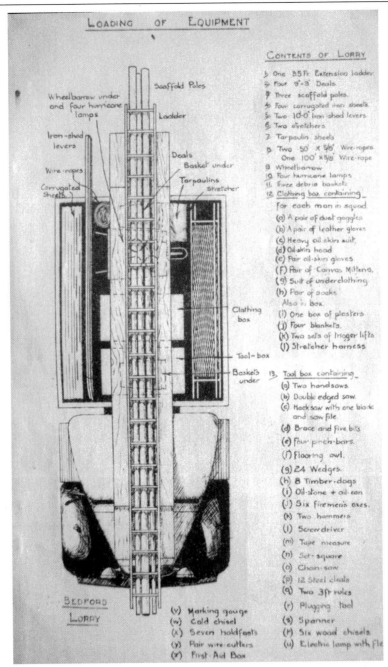

This illustration is taken from the Borough of Bacup's Rescue Training manual, and was drawn by Alan Foster. It demonstrates the meticulous detail which went into the preparation and planning of rescue work.

BOROUGH OF ACCRINGTON

COMBINED BOMBING & SABOTAGE EXERCISE

An Exercise of the above nature will be held in the Borough tomorrow (Sunday) between the hours of 8 and 11 o'clock in the morning in which the co-operation of the public is cordially invited, particularly in those areas where they may see Civil Defence and Home Guard operations in progress.

It will be much appreciated if members of the public will fall in with the wishes of the responsible officers of those areas where their services are needed, and, as some guidance in this direction, the following information can be given:–

1. Umpires, from whom directions can be taken and to whom any information may be given, will wear a white handkerchief on the left arm.

2. 'Enemy' troops will wear forage caps with flaps down.

3. Own troops will wear steel helmets.

Anything the public can do to hinder the enemy troops and infuse some realism into the Exercise will be much appreciated.

Part of the Exercise will call for the opening of certain Rest Centres and the public in the areas concerned are particularly urged to proceed in as large numbers as possible to such centres in order that this service may be fully tested under conditions as near as possible to those that would be created as a result of actual bombing.

Warning as to Messages.

The public are warned that should it be necessary to telephone any real message to the Police Station during the period of the Exercise, special care must be taken to ensure that the recipient of the message does not identify it with the Exercise.

W.H. WARHURST.
Town Clerk.

Town Hall,
Accrington.

Unfortunately the date this exercise was held is not known. The original notice is too damaged to reproduce.

Bullough's Rescue Squad practise casualty evacuation outside the workers' canteen on Ormerod Street, Accrington, 1940.

Staff of the Barrage Balloon HQ, which was based at Accrington. Barrage balloons were flown near factories doing essential war work. Some of them occasionally broke free; one was found wrapped round the chimney of Premier Mill, Great Harwood. Work in the mill had to be stopped as the balloon had been punctured by the mill's lightning conductor and gas was escaping. The balloon was eventually released by a steeplejack, but not before it had weakened the chimney, which had to be bound by iron rings for safety.

Section Three

THE HOME GUARD

The Home Guard commenced life as the Local Defence Volunteers, a body of men whose purpose was to defend their homes and families in case of invasion. Ex-Servicemen were asked to join along with any other men between the ages of 16 and 60. Organized into platoons, companies and battalions, the men were issued with khaki armbands bearing the initials LDV, which were soon understood to stand for 'Look, Duck and Vanish', as the men were initially armed with nothing more than sticks. Morale was greatly improved when they were issued with a small number of rifles. This enabled companies such as 'C' Company at Rawtenstall, which received six rifles, to begin making Dawn and Dusk patrols; one rifle, carried by an ex-serviceman, went with each patrol of six men, along with five rounds of ammunition carried in a sealed box.

In May 1940 Winston Churchill changed the name of the LDV to the Home Guard, soon after which the men were issued with denim uniforms. These were eventually to be replaced by khaki, and a more professional appearance was given when army boots, other equipment, and more rifles and bayonets were issued.

Men, young and old, working and retired, spent many hours learning a variety of new skills. Less time was spent on formation marching and more time given to practical purposes such as weapons training and tactics. To prepare for an invasion, exercises were carried out on the hills, where a lot of fighting was thought likely to take place, and dummy attacks on other towns were practised, sometimes against other Home Guard units, and later against the Regular Army, to help the latter on its return to the battlegrounds of Europe.

After the evacuation of Dunkirk, there was a serious threat that German troops would be landing on British home territory, but this receded after the Battle of Britain. On 5 November 1940 Churchill referred both to the state of the Home Guard and the invasion:

When I spoke at the end of June, I set forth in detail the well-known difficulties which would attend the invasion of these islands, and which had been forgotten in years when we had not considered the matter at all. At the time we had only a few brigades of well-armed and well-trained troops in this island. We had no Home Guard to deal with an invader or to deal with airborne attacks behind the lines, and the Royal Air Force had not then proved itself master of our own air by daylight. Very different is the scene today. We have a large Army here, improving in equipment and training continually. The main part of the Army is now highly mobile, and is being constantly imbued with the spirit of counter-attack. We have 1,700,000 in the Home Guard, all of whom will be in uniform by the end of this year, and nearly all of whom are in uniform at this moment. Nearly 1,000,000 of the Home Guard have rifles or machine-guns. Nearly half of the Home Guard are veteran soldiers of the last war. Such a force is of the highest value and importance. A country where every street and every village bristles with loyal and resolute armed men is a country against which the kind of tactics which destroyed Dutch resistance – tactics of parachutists or airborne troops in carriers or gliders, Fifth Column activities, if there were any over here, and I am increasingly sceptical – a country so defended would not be liable to be overthrown by such tactics.

As the tide of the war changed, members of the Home Guard realized that once the European invasion was on, Britain would only be defended by the Home Guard. In his diary, James Melia, an ex-serviceman in the First World War who had risen to be a Major in the Home Guard, in charge of 'C' Company, Rawtenstall, recalled what happened when D-Day was announced:

One morning the newspapers came out with glaring headlines, 'Allies landing in Normandy', with descriptions of various newswriters who were eyewitnesses. I went down to 'C' Coy in the evening, and although not a day usually detailed for parade or training, almost the whole company was there, waiting to see what they could do. It was staggering to say the least.

The successes of the invasion force made it obvious that the protection of volunteers was no longer required, and on 3 December 1944 the Home Guard was disbanded. James Melia recalled:

Christmas 1944 was the end of the Home Guard. A dinner was held to celebrate four years' service and good fun, but we didn't forget those who had served with us and then fought in the fiercer battles on the Continent; many of those never returned, but as in the spirit of the First World War, they were remembered mostly by those who loved them best. It was announced on the news over the radio that the Minister of War would make a speech of thanks to all members of the Home Guard. He did, and to all who listened to it, the feeling was that he told us he thanked us for our services, now get out of uniform and get on with your business. Many references to the crudeness of his remarks were in the following day's newspapers, but the members of the Home Guard, although bitterly disappointed, just carried on.

'C' Company, Rawtenstall Home Guard, wearing civvies, preparing for a trip out on a Ben Barnes' coach.

'C' Company, Rawtenstall Home Guard, in uniform. Back row, left to right: -?-, -?-, Walter Hoyle, Billy Fearnley, Bob Green, -?-. Front row: Johnny Hampson, Tom Flannery, Stanley Green (Army Cadet), -?-.

'C' Company, Rawtenstall Home Guard, Drum Band. Left to right: D. Wildman, E. Royal, A. Walton, J. Horrocks (Drum Major), K. Edmondson, N. Woodbine, J. Guinea, J. Clegg. James Melia noted in his diary:

'C' Coy had an excellent drum band trained by a Corporal Drummer of the Regular Army who had finished his time just before the outbreak of war. The boys were exceedingly smart, and when on the march attracted the attention of the public by their smartness and very clean equipment. It was a treat to march behind them. Major Grindley was the prime mover in their organisation and funds for their maintenance was mainly his duty to find. He did this by begging from the people in the town who could afford small gifts. Capt. Worswick MC of the First World War gave £100 towards them, but wouldn't join the Home Guard; he thought he was too old.

No. 1 Platoon, Blackburn Home Guard, 10th Lancashire Battalion on manoeuvres near New Inns, Blackburn, November 1941.

Pillbox at Catlow, near Burnley, 1974. A number of these remain standing in East Lancashire. During the war they were manned by members of the Home Guard.

Ramsbottom Home Guard outside the Drill Hall, Crow Lane, Ramsbottom.

Members of Nelson Home Guard, making practical use of empty buildings. It was expected that in the event of an invasion every street and house might have to be fought for.

Although the Home Guard is largely remembered as a voluntary service, on 15 December 1941 a White Paper giving details of the Government proposals for the reorganization of the Home Guard was published. These included compulsory enrolment for men between 18 and 55 in areas where an insufficient number of men were forthcoming under the voluntary system; volunteers to the Home Guard lost their right to resign at fifteen days' notice; a Home Guard who absented himself, without reasonable excuse, from parade or duty, would be liable to penalties, and the maximum period of training was to be fixed for the time being at 48 hours, spread over a four-week period.

Whitworth Home Guard.

Members of Accrington Home Guard. Back row, left to right: W. Johnson, who had a paper shop in Park Street, -?-, Mr Cunliffe, who worked at Broad Oak Mill, Mr Finch, Cyril Holditch, who worked at Broad Oak Mill, and later emigrated to Australia. Front row: -?-, Mr Drake, Mr McKinley, who worked at Broad Oak Mill, Mr Bradbury, who worked at Broad Oak Mill.

Blackburn Home Guard, 10th Lancashire Battalion, outside the Technical College, Blackburn. Major Bilsborrow was the Commanding Officer and Peter Duckworth second in command. Lt. Richard Slater of No. 1 Platoon is fourth from the right in the front row.

Blackburn Home Guard, No. 1 Mobile Company, 10th Lancashire Battalion, outside the Technical College.

'F' Company, Burnley Home Guard, outside the Drill Hall, Keighley Green, *c*. 1942. An extract from James Melia's diary reads:

> There was humour as well as work; they told of one of the boys on sentry duty who, when the Duty Officer approached, challenged with, 'Halt, who am I?' Then, of course, there was the story of the challenge, 'Halt, who goes there?', and the donkey braying back at him. Then there was the cow shot dead by the sentry because it didn't know the password in the dark.

Members of the Home Guard, Nelson.

Ramsbottom Home Guard.

Tottington Home Guard.

After the 'Stand Down' a certificate, bearing the title of the Home Guard and the signature of the King, was presented to every member who served, stating his name and the period he served. The certificate read:

In the years when our Country was in mortal danger Tommy Atkins who served 21 April 1941–31 Dec, 1944 gave generously of his time and powers to make himself ready for her defence by force of arms and with his life if need be.

Officers of 10th County Battalion Blackburn Home Guard, outside the Technical College, preparing for 'Stand Down' in December 1944. Part of the King's speech, on 3 December 1944, was as follows:

It was well known to the enemy that if he came to any part of our land he would meet determined opposition, at every point in his advance, from men who had good weapons and, better still, knew how to use them. In that way the existence of the Home Guard helped much to ward off the danger of invasion. Then, too, our own plans for campaigns in many parts of the world depended on our having a great citizen force to help in the defence of the homeland. As anti-aircraft and coastal gunners, sentries at vulnerable points, units for dealing with unexploded bombs, and in many other ways, the Home Guard have played a full part in the defence of their country.

I am very proud of what the Home Guard has done and I give my heartfelt thanks to you all. Officers, non-commissioned officers, and men, you have served your country with a steadfast devotion. I know that your country will not forget that service.

MUNITIONS

Although the budget for munitions and armaments had been increased several times both before and during the early part of the war, it was not until Winston Churchill's elevation to the position of Prime Minister in May 1940 that a substantial effort was made to increase the output of equipment with which to fight the battle. The Government's initial rally cry, coined by the new Minister of Supply, Herbert Morrison, was 'Go to it'. On 30 May 1940 he put his case to the country:

> I have been called to direct one part of that effort which falls to us here at home. The Ministry of Supply inherits in large measure the task that was performed in the last war by the Ministry of Munitions. The job of my Ministry is to turn the wealth of the nation into bullets, and shells, and guns, and tanks; to take the raw material of our great productive power and forge it into a sword of victory. Now that the full pressure of war is upon us, the drive behind the work must increase. Its pace must quicken. Its scope must extend. More shells, more tanks, more guns: these are the swords that we can place in the hands of our brave sons, the shields that we can throw before their bodies.

Much vitally needed equipment had been lost in the retreat from France in 1940. This not only had to be replaced, but added to on a great scale. As the situation on the Continent grew worse, it became apparent that Britain might be left alone in Europe, but every day that passed the capacity to manufacture weapons grew, with workers urged on to greater efforts, as usual by posters asking them to 'Work at War Speed'.

New factories had been built in the north-west, and old textile mills either closed or converted their production lines to the manufacture of supplies necessary for the war effort. Factories which before the war had made consumer goods found themselves being retooled and the workforce, depleted by war service and added to by unskilled employees, was retrained to work on the new machines. In the relatively safe industrial areas of Lancashire, bombs, shells, aircraft, parachutes, boots, uniforms and many other commodities vital to the war effort were made and dispatched to the fighting forces.

Despite the renewed efforts to increase production, in July 1941 there was much criticism of how the Government was managing the affairs of the nation. There was a long debate on war production, with widespread publicity given to a statement that the country was only working at 75 per cent of full efficiency. An indication of exactly how hard people were working was given in Churchill's scathing response to the criticism:

Seventy-five per cent of what? I have tried to find a datum line, and took the three months after Dunkirk. Then our people worked to the utmost limit of their strength. There was a great spurt in June, July, and August of last year. This produced an altogether abnormal inflation of production. If we take those three months as the datum line, is it true that we are only working to seventy-five percent of that? There were several reasons why we could not maintain indefinitely the intense efforts of the past year; workers must have reasonable minimum holidays – at least one week's holiday in the year; Sunday work had been practically eliminated – and necessarily so; allowances had to be made for the very severe change in the diet of the heavy manual worker.

In 1942 over a million more men were engaged in making munitions than in the previous war, whilst the mobilization of women was on an unprecedented and unrivalled scale.

In 1943 it was reported that men in the munitions factories were working over 55 hours a week, and women over 50 hours. To these hours should be added the time spent on all the other duties, such as fire-watching, which were either demanded or expected. On top of all this were the added pressures caused by members of the family or friends being away in the armed forces where they were at risk of being wounded, killed or captured; the restrictions of rationing; demands to work harder; the threat of air raids; and the war news, which for so long was nothing but dismal.

This photograph shows the management and some of the staff of S.S. Stott Ltd, Haslingden, who manufactured fuses and shells for the war effort. The management included Harry Rishton, Mr Davies and Harry Knott. The male workers were: John Shaw, Jack Mays, Mr Melia, Fred Brown, John Entwistle, Harry Nuttall, Mr Dobson and electrician, Ned Collinge. Amongst the girls were Dorothy Mead, Alice Kelly, Mrs Pilkington, Nellie Pilling, Nora Vizzard, Annie Vizzard, Nellie Newhey, Margaret Trickett, Marjorie Burnett, Joyce Howarth, Annie Evans, Elsie Warburton, Winnie Street, Nellie Horan, Elsie Crowther, Florence Haworth and her sister, May Manning, Joan Mason, Joan Donaldson, May Walsh, Kathleen McNamee, May Cardwell, Lillian Rigg, Eileen Nuttall, Alice Killingbeck, Hilda Walsh, Elsie Hatton, Doris Nuttall, Eileen Bentley, Connie Mead, Rene Ireland, Kathleen Adlum, May Westwell, Joan Bailey, Mrs Hamer and Nellie Sorenson.

The management and more of the employees of S.S. Stott Ltd.

An interior photograph of S.S. Stott Ltd, showing a group of the girls with some of the munitions they had made.

A fancy dress fund-raising group of young women and men who worked at S.S. Stott's foundry in Haslingden, with a poster saying 'Give us the brass, we'll make the rings.' Some recollections of how they coped are given by Elsie Tattersall, a mill girl who started working on munitions at S.S. Stott Ltd at the beginning of the war, and remained there for the duration, often working twelve-hour shifts:

> We had no canteen at Stott's, only an old gas oven in which you could warm a dinner or a potato in its jacket, but only at lunchtime. There was also a Women's Voluntary Service canteen at St Peter's Church close by, and any workers could go – it was one shilling for a good lunch. We had to make do with a little them days, clothes and stockings all on coupons. Some with big families could not afford to use all the coupons so they wanted to sell them. It was very dark going to work in those days, no lights at all and some of us girls used to meet up and go to work together. If you had a torch, which most had, you had to cover it with paper and leave just a little hole in the centre. The toilets were a long way off and we dared not go on our own – we had to go in groups. Every Friday the two shifts would have a collection for the soldiers. Also, we used to save ship halfpennies which we sent to the *Observer*. If you gave the newspaper the names of the soldiers they would send them some cigarettes which was nice of them. In war time everyone helped as best they could. We did our best at organizing the processions to help the boys fighting for us and collecting money for treats for them.

Horsa rib assembly, Co-operative Wholesale Society Cabinet Works, Radcliffe.

As in thousands of other factories, the war brought great changes to this works, which previously had been engaged in the manufacture of cabinets and wooden furniture. After the outbreak of hostilities, the Government ordered many of the CWS factories to produce urgent items such as ammunition and food boxes, beds, and air raid shelter bunks. It was not long, however, before more complex items were required. Factories were redirected to manufacture components for aircraft such as fuselages, wings and nose cones for the Horsa gliders and Mosquito aeroplanes. In addition, the CWS factory at Radcliffe also manufactured over 8,000 collapsible boats.

Between 40 and 50 per cent of the workers were women who before the war had been typists, mill workers and shop assistants. They had little or no mechanical experience but quickly learned to handle machinery and perform laborious tasks.

The manufacture of domestic furniture was prohibited from 1 November 1942, except for Utility furniture, introduced from 1 January 1943. Free of purchase tax, it was obtainable under permit on a 'units' system, by newly married couples, anyone who had been bombed out, and from 26 March by families with children setting up house for the first time. Couples with no furniture were entitled to 60 units, and an additional 15 units for each child. Unit values of furniture included: sideboard, 8; table, 6; dining chair, 1; fireside chair, 5. Nursery furniture could be bought without restrictions, when available.

Aircraft depot main assembly at the Cooperative Wholesale Society Cabinet Works, Radcliffe.

Loading a Horsa glider wing at the Cooperative Wholesale Society Cabinet Works, Radcliffe.

Glue spreading at the Cooperative Wholesale Society Cabinet Works, Radcliffe.

Tape jointing at the Cooperative Wholesale Society Cabinet Works, Radcliffe.

Mrs Mary Smithson and Doris Moore in the lead-lined room containing an X-ray machine at Lupton and Place Ltd, Burnley. Before the war Mary had worked in a shop until transferring to war production. In addition to working on the X-ray machine, she also spent some time in the machine shop, filing and drilling, as well as pressure testing castings.

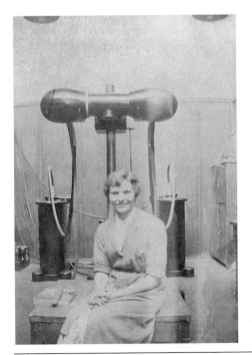

A friend of Mrs Smithson, Vera Davy, with the X-ray machine at Lupton and Place Ltd, Burnley. The machine was used for the testing of castings for aircraft, including the Hurricane and Spitfire. In total six girls worked the X-ray machine on a rota system, on occasions having to keep the work going 24 hours a day.

Women munition workers at Bulloughs in Accrington. The shortage of manpower meant that for the first time women were employed there, apart from in the office. The first girl on the left is Dorothy Riley, and the last girl is Frances Wilkinson, née Riley, donor of the photograph.

Adrian Lombard's design team at Barnoldswick celebrating at a dinner party given by Rolls-Royce, after the Derwent V jet engine had set the first post-war speed record (and first jet world speed record) in the Gloster Meteor at 606 m.p.h. at Herne Bay in Kent. The photograph was taken at the Black Bull, Rimington, September 1945. Back row, left to right: William Carnegie, -?-, Ralph Janes, Gordon Morley, Arthur Bill, John Bill, Adrian Lombard, Christopher Davies, Ewan Davies, Fred Morley, Stan Wilkins, Terry Gardiner, Ron Charlton, Dennis Bacon, John Moore. Front row: Steve Langham, Jim Simpson, Sam Whiteley, Jean ?, Freda ?, John Bush, Dick Gillespie.

In the middle of the Second World War a group of men had met in Clitheroe's Swan and Royal Hotel. These men were discussing an invention which would give us command of the skies. Maurice Wilks of Rover Motor Group, Stanley Hooker, a man brought in by Rolls-Royce, and Ernest Hives of Rolls-Royce were round the table to discuss the top secret project of the jet engine. The development sites were at Waterloo Mill, Clitheroe, and Bankfield Mill, Barnoldswick. The project had been delayed by squabbles and the Rover Group withdrew from the project. The Clitheroe base was used for research and development and Barnoldswick was used for the production of the engine. The Clitheroe-produced W2B engine was tested for the first time in the tail of a Wellington bomber.

Joseph Lucas Ltd was contracted to produce and develop the fuel system and combustion chamber. Many apprentices from Clitheroe were employed on this project.

Rolls-Royce Test Department, Bankfield, Clitheroe/Barnoldswick, 1948, showing many of the team who were involved with the development of the jet engine. Back row, left to right: H. Stanworth, W.H. Riggs, T. Lancaster, R. Wilkinson, H. Fennel, B. Hurt, A. Gupwell, S.M. Rushworth, A. Fawcett, W. Burgess, J. Bell. Middle row: G. Fox, J. Weightman, H. Hobbs, J. Cubbins, J. Johnson, K. Smith, T. Grimshaw, W. Harvey, D. Beaty, H. Child, R.F. Wilkinson, W.V. Leake, N. Dutton, L. Harper, H. Isles, J. Snape, I. Clapham. Front row: Mrs G. Carter, Miss N. Shaw, Miss O. Coates, S. Smith, E.D. Wye, S. Kay, C.D. Davidson, W.B. Harling, N.R. Houlgate, P.H. Smith, Mrs E. MacLean, Mrs M. Patterson, Miss A. Duxbury, Miss J. Sanders.

Some members of the team that helped develop the jet engine are seen here at a 1993 reunion held at the Rolls-Royce Welfare Centre. Jack Gregory of Lucas, Eric Edmondson, Jimmy Hoyle (now sadly deceased), and Frank Eccles are among those present.

This display stand was erected just after the war had ended by A.C. Cossor Ltd, of Wren Mill, Chadderton. Originally based in Mitcham, Surrey, the company was bombed out and relocated to a cotton mill in Chadderton. The new Production Manager, Ernest Pollard, who now lives in Great Harwood, recalled that the security was so great he did not know that his work was as important as it was. In fact the mill was making top secret 'Gee' equipment which was fitted into aircraft, and was one of the many developments of RADAR – 'Radio Location and Ranging'. The 'Gee' instruments could pick up one-way radar impulses emitted from ground stations. From these LORAN (Long Range Air Navigation) signals, navigators within the aircraft could plot their position rapidly and accurately. The task of the RAF to organize mass bombing raids over enemy territory was made possible by the use of 'Gee'. Mr Pollard recalls that some of the equipment was even modified to be used on camels and donkeys.

Cannons being removed for salvage from the Coppice, Accrington. After the First World War, a large number of enemy weapons had been distributed throughout the country to be placed in memorial gardens and places of prominence. Somewhat ironically, those that had been left in place until the Second World War were removed to be melted down and used in Britain's war effort.

Section Five

WAR WEAPONS' LOANS

By March 1940 the cost of financing the war had reached £4,000,000 a day, a figure which by February 1941 had risen to over £11,000,000 a day. By April 1943 the war had cost £13,000,000,000 and reached a daily expenditure of £15,000,000. The tremendous strain on the economy was reflected in the wartime budgets which, amongst many other stringent measures, introduced Purchase Tax and increased Income Tax to 50 per cent.

To help fund the cost of the war, a War Savings campaign was started, which by 1940 had reached a total of £100,000,000, made up of Defence Bonds and War Savings. The Government strove to encourage the campaign by every means available, but one of the most popular ways of appealing to the patriotism of the people was the introduction of local campaigns lasting a week with a specific theme, such as 'Wings for Victory', 'Spitfire Week', and 'Warship Week'.

A great deal of organization went into making a fund-raising week successful. Great Harwood's 'War Weapons' Week' had an executive committee of eight, and the chairmen and secretaries of the various other committees, which included Bonds and Finance, Industrial, Tradesmen's, Schools and Churches, Events and Publicity, and a Ladies' Committee. In total, over one hundred people were members of at least one committee.

An example of the wide variety of the organizations which took part in a typical week-long fund raising campaign can be ascertained from the official programme of Great Harwood's 'Salute the Soldier Week', which took place between 3 and 10 June 1944.

The opening ceremony held on Saturday 3 June was performed by the Rt. Hon. Lord Shuttleworth, who also took the salute at the March Past, accompanied by Sir William Brass MP, Sir Reginald Blaker, Bart, MP, Captain A.F. Hordern, Chief Constable of the County, A.S. Kershaw, Esq., and members of the District Council and Executive Committee. The parade was led by the Band of the Lancashire Fusiliers and the order of the procession was: Army, American Army, Home Guard, ATS, ACF, ATC, British Legion, Police and Special Constabulary, Air Raid Wardens, Bristol Aeroplane Company's band, St John Ambulance Brigade and Nursing Division, NFS, Rescue Squad, First Aid Post and Girl Guides.

Each day the Indicator Ceremony took place, performed by the representatives of different groups.

No events took place on the Sunday, but on Monday there was an exhibition of Rolls-Royce engines held in the canteen of Messrs Rolls-Royce Ltd, Britannia Street, repeated on Tuesday and Wednesday. Admission was by the purchase of a Saving Stamp, though members of the armed forces in uniform were admitted free. In the evening there was also a joint exhibition given on the Football Ground, Lowerfold Park, by members of the Home Guard, Army Cadet Force, First Aid, Casualty, and other Civil Defence Services.

On Tuesday a Royal Engineers' travelling circus, consisting of a tank, bulldozer and wagons fitted to display bridge building equipment, together with small landing craft, set up a display on Haydock Square and Britannia Street Lodge, from 2 p.m. to dusk. In the evening, entertainment was given in Mercer Hall, provided by Rolls-Royce employees.

Wednesday afternoon saw a garden fête held in Lowerfold Park, with dances, music, a variety troupe, fortune tellers and stall, and a selling centre for the sale of Certificates and Stamps. In the evening a children's fancy dress ball was held in Mercer Hall, and a cricket match between the Home Guard and Civil Defence was held on the Red Lane ground.

On Thursday the Indicator Ceremony was performed at 12.15 p.m. by schoolchildren, who then listened to a talk by A.S. Kershaw. In the evening the ATC gave a demonstration of memory drill and physical training, followed by the cadets' musical show.

On Friday a Grand Ball was held in Mercer Hall with dancing from 8 p.m. to 1 a.m. to the music of Eddie McGarry's Dance Band. On Saturday 10 June, just the Indicator Ceremony was performed, as was the case on Monday 12 June, when the final total was announced.

Not only did all the activities of the campaign for War Loans raise money with which to pursue the war, they also performed the great service of strengthening the bonds between those on the Home Front and the armed forces.

The amount of money raised by Burnley for its 'War Weapons' Loans Week' was shown publicly on a chimney indicator. This was 30 ft high and erected on the site of the old John Taylor & Co. Ltd, wine and spirit merchant at the corner of Yorkshire Street and Church Street.

MAKE YOUR MONEY FIGHT

BY SAVING AND LENDING. THE MIGHTY WEAPONS OF DEFENCE AND ATTACK WILL HELP TO WIN THE WAR. LEND YOUR MONEY TO PAY FOR THEM NOW.

This 'Make Your Money Fight' leaflet was one of many issued by the National Savings Committee, to encourage people to invest in National Savings Stamps to help finance the war effort. With the banner heading 'Save and Lend for Victory', the leaflet exhorted: 'Make your money fight. We want more weapons and yet more weapons of defence and attack. Save and lend to pay for them now.'

The leaflet also gave the individual approximate cost of a variety of weapons and equipment: bomber aircraft £20,000, fighter aircraft £5,000, barrage balloon £700, searchlight projector £1,500, battleship £8,000,000, aircraft carrier £3,300,000, cruiser £2,000,000, large destroyer £450,000, small destroyer £320,000, submarine £350,000, guns, mountings and turrets for nine 16-inch naval guns £3,000,000, torpedo £2,000, medium tank £15,000, heavy AA gun £6,000, light AA gun £3,000, small gun £1,500, spare gun barrel £500, heavy AA shell £4, machine-gun £100, heavy machine-gun £350, a mortar £40, cost of equipping an infantry soldier with 184 items including gas mask and rifle £20, service rifle £7, 1,000 rounds of rifle ammunition £5 10s. 0d., service pistol £4, and hand grenade 4s.

HMS *Moonstone*, the ship adopted by Whitworth and District, was a trawler minesweeper, costing £62,000. It had been launched in 1934 and was broken up in 1946. Amongst its many exploits, it took a leading part in the capture of a U-boat in 1940. In 1994 the ship's plaque was presented to Whitworth Historical Society, and now hangs on the wall of the museum in Whitworth.

HMS *Fancy*, an Algerine-class Fleet Minesweeper, with a crew of 110 officers and men, was the adopted ship of Rawtenstall. She was the ninth ship of that name in the Royal Navy, the first having been a hired pinnace which took part in the action against the Armada in 1588. Of about 1,000 tons displacement, she was armed with a single 4 inch gun, four single 20 mm Oerlikons and depth charges, and equipped with Radar and Asdic. The minesweeping gear comprised Oropesa gear for moored mines, LL electric cable for magnetic mines and SA hammer and Fessenden Oscillator for acoustic mines.

Commissioned in November 1943, HMS *Fancy* helped to clear ten channels through the German minefield for the invasion fleet in June 1944. More minesweeping off Normandy and the North Sea, and some repairs, took up the rest of the year. In 1945 she was prepared to go to the Far East via Gibraltar and Malta, where she was re-allocated to the 19th MSF in the Mediterranean, followed by service in the Adriatic, clearing channels to Venice and Trieste. During this time one of the ships in the fleet was sunk, HMS *Coriolanus*, another locally adopted ship. After more sweeping off the coast of Greece, HMS *Fancy* returned to her home port of Chatham, and was then sent to Cuxhaven to supervise German minesweepers clearing minefields off Norway. During her time the *Fancy* accounted for 250 mines. After being re-allocated to a training flotilla at Portsmouth she was placed in reserve, until transferred in 1951 to the Belgian Navy and renamed *A.F. Dufour*. Used both for minesweeping and training, she took part in the Belgian Congo campaign and renamed *N'zadi*. When the Belgians left the Congo, the ship was left stranded at Banana, where she still remains as a desolate hulk.

The spending of money on anything other than necessities and War Savings was considered to be thriftless, hence this 'Squander Bugs' poster, which utilized the talents of cartoonists to put across the message.

The SS *Hazel*, named after Nicholas Worsley Ltd's Hazel Mill, Haslingden. The banner reads 'GET THE COUNTRY SHIP SHAPE – KEEP ON SAVING'. The display was in aid of Haslingden's 'Wings for Victory Week'.

The prow of a mock-up ship, HMS *Pearl*, erected to encourage investment in Savings Bonds, during Padiham and District's 'Warships' Week', 21–8 February 1942. The intention was to raise enough money to cover the cost of a Trawler Minesweeper. The target was £62,000, to cover the cost of the hull (£40,000), main auxiliary machinery (£19,000), armament and munitions (£1,700), other equipment (£1,300). The final figure raised in this week was actually £122,000. From left to right: an unknown serviceman, Jackson Sagar, Mrs Bradshaw, Thomas Wright Waddington, Mrs Williams, Percy Williams, Clerk of the Council, Superintendent Pickering, Councillor Ernest Bradshaw, Chairman of the Council.

Such was the bond that developed between Padiham and members of the crew of the *Pearl*, that even fifty years later veterans of the Navy still return to the town annually.

Parade and March Past for the 'Wings For Victory Week' held in Haslingden on Saturday 29 May 1944. The Women's Auxiliary Air Force was approved by the King on 2 July 1939. On 13 February 1948 the Women's Service Bill was passed by MPs, which made the WAAF permanent, but to be known as the Women's Royal Air Force.

Blackburn Home Guard at the 'Wings for Victory' Parade, spring 1943. This photograph shows No. 1 Mobile Company in the March Past, passing the post office in Darwen Street, Blackburn.

A fighter plane on display during 'Wings for Victory Week', on Broadway, Accrington, with the Market Hall in the background.

This photograph of a car with a model of a Spitfire on top was taken in the yard of Accrington Fire Station. The board attached to one side of the car reads 'Buy a Spitfire to shoot the Nazis down'; on the other side the board reads 'Civil Defence Spitfire Fund'.

A Spitfire bought by local people, 1940. The names of the towns, Accrington, Church and Oswaldtwistle, are written on the side of the plane beneath the cockpit.

There is a story that in one Oswaldtwistle mill that had been turned over to the production of aircraft, the boffins were having problems with a new type of aeroplane, which, although very good in most respects, had a serious problem. Every time it tried to take to the air its wings fell off, and the boffins were at a loss what to do. However, an old tackler suggested that they should drill small holes into the wings where they joined the fuselage. In desperation they tried the suggestion, and it worked. Amazed by their success, the boffins asked the tackler where he had learned his great knowledge of aerodynamics. 'I know nowt about that', he replied, 'I got th' idea when I were i' toilet. That damn paper never tears along t' little 'oyles.'

A Spitfire fitted with cannon. Although the Spitfire is the best remembered of fighter aircraft, the Hawker Hurricane and Boulton-Paul Defiant also played their part in what was to become known as the Battle of Britain. In 1941 a pamphlet issued by the Ministry of Information on behalf of the Air Ministry told the story of the battle, which commenced on 8 August 1940, when the Germans launched the first of a series of mass air attacks in daylight on the United Kingdom. The pamphlet records Winston Churchill's speech to the House of Commons on 20 August 1940:

> After referring to the work and achievements of the Navy, Mr Winston Churchill turned to the war in the air. 'The gratitude of every home in our island,' he said, 'in our Empire and indeed throughout the world, except in the abodes of the guilty, goes out to the British airmen, who, undaunted by odds, unwearied in their constant challenge and mortal danger, are turning the tide of world war by their prowess and by their devotion. Never in the field of human conflict was so much owed by so many to so few.'
>
> The Prime Minister was speaking at a moment when the battle was still at its height, for it was not until the end of October that the German Luftwaffe virtually abandoned its attacks by daylight and began to rely entirely on a policy of night raiding – its tacit admission of defeat. Between 8th August and 31st October 2,375 German aircraft are known to have been destroyed in daylight. This figure takes no account of those lost at night or those, seen by thousands, staggering back to their French bases, wings and fuselage full of holes, ailerons shot away, engines smoking and dripping glycol, undercarriages dangling – the retreating remnants of a shattered and disordered Armada. This melancholy procession of the defeated was to be observed not once but many times during those summer and autumn days of 1940. Truly it was a great deliverance.
>
> It was not achieved without cost. The Royal Air Force lost 375 pilots killed and 358 wounded. Such was the Battle of Britain in 1940. Future historians may compare it with Marathon, Trafalgar and the Marne.

Clitheroe Borough and Rural District 'Warships' Week', 21–8 March 1942. This shows the final ceremony in Market Place.

The parade for Clitheroe Borough and Rural District 'Warships' Week.'

The parade for Clitheroe Borough and Rural District 'Warships' Week.'

Gen. Sir George Cooper reviewing the Royal Engineers in 1991 on the Castle Grounds at Clitheroe, which had been dedicated as a War Memorial after the First World War.

The review was one of a number of events which took place to commemorate the fiftieth anniversary of the establishment of No. 1 Training Battalion, Royal Engineers in 1941. Low Moor Mill had been converted into a barracks, and sappers from all over the country and from abroad came for training. The prototype of the Bailey bridge was erected in Clitheroe, a small model which was tested by two local boys who later emigrated to Australia. The bridge itself was used in many theatres of war, and the longest, about 1,000 yd, was erected in Burma.

The River Ribble provided a good site for testing bridges as well as weapons. Now resident in Clitheroe, Brinley Joynson, who was a sergeant in the RE and spent some time with the battalion, recalls one instance when all did not go well:

> One day I was told that the RAF would be practising an attack on a pontoon bridge and, having been trained in small arms, I would be firing a Bren Gun into the banking with live ammunition as there wasn't enough blank ammo to use for that! The river had been prepared with charges of gelignite, in a row down the bank sides. These were wired so that they could be individually exploded as the Spitfire planes flew over. On the day I was looking away from the river and as the planes flew down from Bungerley I started to fire into the little hillside. Suddenly there was an almighty bang and all the charges went off together, in front of the Spitfires. Chunks of stone hurtled into the air and one plane had a hole blown through its port wing. We learned afterwards that the RAF were not amused, especially the pilot.

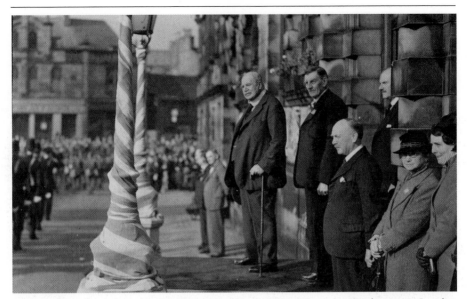

Lord Derby taking the salute at Great Harwood's 'War Weapons' Week', 3–11 October 1941, on the steps of the Town Hall. A week of activities was organized to encourage the citizens to raise a target figure of £50,000 in Savings Certificates, but the amount raised was £176,723.

GREAT HARWOOD

"Salute the Soldier" Week

3rd June to 10th June, 1944.

OUR TARGET

£60,000.

TANKS——Our aim is FOUR
But we must get more!

OFFICIAL PROGRAMME.

Price · · · · 2d.

Official programme of Great Harwood's 'Salute the Soldier Week', 3–10 June 1944. The opening ceremony was performed by the 4th Lord Shuttleworth, who came to the title in 1941. His two uncles, the only sons of the 1st Lord, had died in service during the First World War. After the 1st Lord's death in 1939, his two cousins, the only grandsons of the 1st Lord, each held the title briefly before perishing in battle, the elder in 1940 and the younger in 1941. The 4th Lord himself had been lucky to survive the war, having lost one leg and suffered great injury to the other.

Great Harwood's 'Wings for Victory Week' commenced on Saturday 29 May 1943. The savings target was £80,000, enough for two Lancaster bombers. Group Captain Harvey officially opened the event, and said: 'The Allies must have air supremacy so as to continue to hit hard by sea and land. To hoard money in the proverbial stocking is unpatriotic. Air power is the finest cover to save the life of the British Soldier.' The amount of money raised in savings was £145,501, which, added to the amount raised for 'War Weapons' Week', was the equivalent of £27 per head of population.

WOMEN AT WAR

'The real heroes of the war were the women; we knew what was happening to us, they didn't,' is the opinion of one old soldier who had entered France with the British Expeditionary Force and had returned after the fall of Dunkirk. It isn't, however, just the way that women coped with the death of their menfolk or the long separation from them by war, which ought to be remembered, but the many and varied tasks they undertook, and the manner in which they performed them, to help the country achieve victory.

The Home Front provided women with many challenges, not the least keeping a household going and providing the family with meals which were governed by the ration book and the availability of unrationed foodstuffs, which were often in short supply. At different times they also had to cope with clothes rationing, furniture rationing and the non-availability of many household goods. On top of all this there was also the disruption of the house itself, with a shelter or other provision having to be made for air raids, and the nightly chore of ensuring the windows and doors were totally blacked out. To assist the housewife were innumerable suggestions given by the radio, newspapers, posters and leaflets on how to make the best use of food, save fuel, patch sheets and blankets, reinforce children's clothes, make slippers and look after shoes, and many other household chores.

With more and more men being called up into the Armed Forces, there was a shortage of manpower which had to be compensated for by the employment of women. In East Lancashire there was a long tradition of women working in mills and factories, many of which were switched from producing peace-time products to munitions. As time went by even more women were required by law to work; some who had not worked before were rather particular, according to James Melia, who in addition to being a member of the Home Guard, was a foreman in a footwear factory. In his diary he wrote: 'Some of the women who had never been inside a factory were very difficult; in the first place they didn't want to come; when they did, they couldn't start, only on the hours 9 till 4; some wanted a sitting down job, others didn't want to sit down; one woman came and wanted to sit down a bit then stand up a bit; she was told that there were good jobs for her on the fair ground, and that if she sat on a dobby horse, she would be bobbing up and down all day. Needless to say she didn't start work for us.'

Women who wanted to wear a uniform to serve the country had many opportunities for either voluntary work or full-time occupations. The services open to them included the Air Transport Auxiliary Service, the Women's Royal Naval Service, the Women's Auxiliary Territorial Service, the Women's Auxiliary Air Force, the First Aid Nursing Yeomanry, the Civil Nursing Reserve, Entertainments National Service Association, Women's Land Army, the Auxiliary Fire Service (later the National Fire Service), the Women's Voluntary Services and Civil Defence.

Recognition of the many ways in which women served the country was given by Queen Elizabeth on 6 December 1944, when she said that the war could not have been won without the 'magnificent' efforts of the women of Britain. She praised all those who worked for the Civil Defence, the fire, ambulance and police services, and the Women's Voluntary Service.

On 5 April 1940 Lord Woolton, Minister of Food, had said:

Today I am going to call on the women of England to mobilize themselves on the Kitchen Front. It doesn't sound romantic; it doesn't sound grand; it isn't dangerous work – but it is vital to our victory. I want the women of England to go into training for the days which may come when the whole of the staying power of the nation will depend on them being able to keep up the energy and the spirits of the industrial workers of this country by feeding them sufficiently when supplies are difficult, when things they have been accustomed to eat and to use in cooking are no longer available.

Between Lord Woolton's speech and the Queen's speech, the women of England had found much more useful things to do than spend all their time on the Kitchen Front.

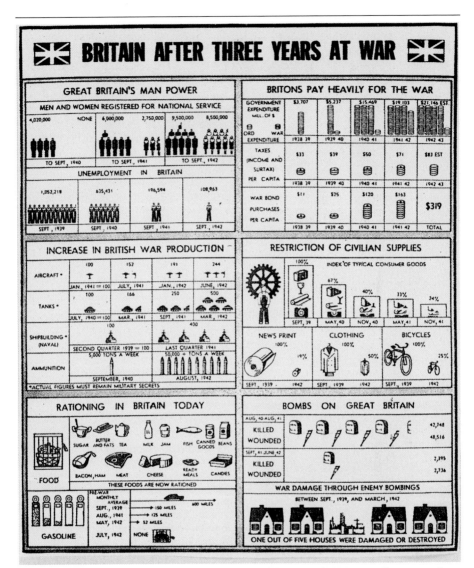

This pictorial chart was issued for distribution in the United States, to show at a glance some of Britain's sacrifices and achievements. The official exchange rate at the time was 4s. 10d. per US dollar, but if the rate is taken at 5s. it will enable a near enough approximation to be made to the American figures shown. The growth of war production was indicated by percentages of the earlier outputs, since actual figures could not be disclosed. The diagram, issued by the British Ministry of Information, gives a general indication of some of the things with which the British housewife had to cope.

Women's Voluntary Service parade at Padiham, May 1941.

National Registration Identity Card. The registration of every adult in the country was carried out not only to ensure that every available man was registered for possible war service, but also every woman. On 2 December 1941 it was announced that all single women between 20 and 30 were to be called up; some were to join anti-aircraft crews along with men, while others would serve in the police and fire service. In total, up to 1,700,000 women were involved in the government's new conscription plans, as the manpower shortage was so acute both in the forces and in the factories. In addition, to meet future needs all women up to 40, both married and single, were to be registered. Boys and girls between 16 and 18 also had to register. It was not until 21 February 1952 that identity cards were abolished.

Women trainee barge crews at Whitebirk, Blackburn, April 1945. On the left of the group are Mrs Mildred Jones, daughter of J.E. Hodson, boatbuilder, who recruited the crews and B.C. Walls, Marine Superintendent.

Out of a total population of 46,750,000 (mid-1942), of whom nine million were children under the age of fourteen, there was an effective population between 14 and 65 of 33,130,000 (15,900,000 males and 17,230,000 females). Of these, 15,200,000 males and 7,100,000 females (including 2,500,000 married women) were in the Services or engaged in full-time paid employment. The remaining 10 million women were married or occupied in necessary household duties. Over a million more men were engaged in making munitions than in the last war, but the mobilization of women was on an unprecedented and unrivalled scale.

On 3 May 1943 a new order was given to make part-time war work compulsory for women of 18 to 45. Previously, about 600,000 people, mostly women, were working part-time (defined as up to 30 hours per week). Each order lasted from three weeks to six months, during which time bosses could not sack workers and workers could not leave other than in exceptional circumstances.

WOMEN'S LAND ARMY

HER ROYAL HIGHNESS THE DUCHESS OF KENT

has graciously consented to present

Fourth Year Armlets at a Party,

to be held in

The School Hall, Eton College
(By kind permission of the Provost)

On Saturday, May 12th, at 3.0 p.m.

The Buckinghamshire County Committee request the

pleasure of the company of

.... *Miss E. Taylor* ....

Please bring this Card with you.

R.S.V.P. County Secretary,
6 St. Mary Street,
High Wycombe.

Eva Taylor's invitation to attend a party to recognize her four years in the Land Army. The production of home-grown food was assisted by thousands of women throughout the country. The Land Army offered a welcome alternative to those women who preferred an outdoor job to office or munition work, or life in the services, such as the WAAF, ATS or WRENS. Members of the Land Army performed every duty required on the farm, and many other jobs, such as working in the timber mills.

Eva Bolton, née Taylor (sadly now
deceased), with her colleagues in the Land
Army, using the basic washing facilities,
and in her Land Army uniform, 1941.

Wedding photograph of Eddie and Martha Collinge. From left to right: Joe and Edna Gent, Eddie and Martha Collinge, Martha's mother, Clara Collinge, and Delia Tennant. Standing behind, on the left, is Harold Collinge.

For entertainment the younger guests went to the pictures, whilst the older ones went for a celebratory drink. Eddie was on a week's leave and a honeymoon was out of the question. Eddie became a Petty Officer and spent some time at HMS *Stag*, a shore base at Port Said. Every month he sent home a selection of tinned fruit to augment the rations. Joe Gent, Eddie's best man, died at sea just six weeks after the photograph was taken.

The wedding of Norman and Phyllis Driver, 26 April 1941, at St Anne's Church, Tottington. The bride, who worked at Kirk Lees' silk works, wore a rose-pink two piece, with brown hat, shoes and gloves. The bridesmaid was Miss Doris Grindrod, a nurse, who was attired in pale blue crêpe georgette with black hat, shoes and gloves. Both these outfits were made up before the introduction of clothing rationing, although women had already been advised by the government to save wood by having flatter heels on their shoes. The best man, James Rushton, was a sheet metal worker and not called up until after the war was over. The groom, a corporal in the Royal Engineers, managed to wangle a new uniform for the ceremony. On 17 June of the previous year he had narrowly escaped death when being evacuated from France after Dunkirk, when HMT *Lancastria*, the ship he was on, was sunk with the loss of approximately 4,000 lives.

This Christmas card, belonging to Mrs Smithson, was sent by her brother, Harry, from Athens in 1944. For some soldiers such as those fighting in the Middle and Far East, the only contact they had with their families for the duration of the war was by post.

This Christmas card from a German POW camp was sent by a soldier who was captured at Calais whilst holding up the German attack on the town in 1940.

CHILDREN AT WAR

For many children in East Lancashire, the pre-war depression had meant poor living conditions, few toys and an inadequate diet. For them, surprisingly, wartime food rationing led to more nourishing meals. The strictures laid down by the ration books, determined measures by the government and the subsidies of certain foodstuffs to keep prices down, ensured a healthier and more balanced diet.

Undoubtedly, with many fathers away in the services for up to six years, or reported dead, missing or captive, and some mothers working long hours in the munition factories, there were many sorrowful and unhappy hours. Small hands and minds, though, could be kept busy, for wartime brought a host of things to do and see which were not available in peacetime.

School lessons were augmented with aircraft recognition and gas mask drill and interrupted by air raid practice, with some children going into shelters carrying a cushion to make the hard seats a little more comfortable, whilst others were taken up on the hillside and told to lie down to avoid bomb blast and shrapnel. During the day, looking out of the classroom windows, children could watch barrage balloons being hoisted high into the air, a reminder of the war. Perhaps, though, the most striking and memorable event for some, was the headmaster reading out the names of past pupils who were reported as dead.

At the commencement of the war even school hours had changed for some, the children attending school in two shifts, morning and afternoon. This was caused by the influx of evacuated children from towns which were thought likely to be attacked by enemy bombers. (Even this dislocation of families provided some humour, a contemporary cartoon showing a small boy saying to his mother: 'Mum, they're going to evacuate me.' The mother replies: 'Oh no they're not. Last time they did that your arm swelled up for a week.')

Out of school, fun could be had watching the Home Guard practice drill and staging mock exercises, seeing foreign soldiers on the streets and searching the sky for aeroplanes.

At home there was the excitement of clambering into the Anderson shelter or hiding under the stairs when the air raid warning sounded, talking to fathers, elder brothers or uncles home on leave, admiring the uniforms and listening to the stories they could tell.

There were also ways in which the children could help the war effort. One Haslingden lady, Sheila McConville, recalls helping to collect salvage and waste paper and being honoured to wear a badge declaring her to be 'A Cog in a Wheel'.

In some towns during 'Warships' Week' a few honoured children were permitted to leave school for a short time to perform the task of adjusting the indicator that showed the amount of money raised in war loans the previous day.

Boys and girls joined the campaign to get the harvests in and to perform other tasks on the farms, called to duty by the posters demanding 'Lend a Hand on the Land'. One of the volunteers was Mrs Sylvia Darwent, of Whitworth, whose father, James William Holt, was an officer in Whitworth Home Guard. She remembers that though the farmers paid for the labour, the money paid didn't go to the children but to the Red Cross, who used it to supply POWs with cigarettes.

Youths were encouraged to joined the Army Cadets and the Air Training Corps, or, when old enough, to join the Home Guard where old but war-tested soldiers imparted much potentially useful knowledge gained from the trenches of the First World War. Girls knitted socks, scarves and gloves for the troops, joined the Guides, helped run the homes, and, along with boys, joined the queues at shops for unrationed food supplies.

Even for the smallest of children there was always something to do, and if there wasn't they could take their lead from the cartoonist who depicted two children, obviously bored. One comes up with the suggestion: 'I know, let's pretend we're Hitler and go and annoy everybody.'

Padiham's favourite dance troupe, the Juvenile Gaieties, was formed by Gladys Hayhurst, a keen amateur dancer who encouraged young girls to take to the stage.

When the war came the Juvenile Gaieties performed in a series of concerts for a host of good causes, including Padiham Aid for Russia, Padiham and District Merchant Navy Week, the Soldiers' Comfort Fund (May 1940), 'Wings for Victory Week' (15–22 May 1943), Earl Haig Poppy Fund (1944), United Aid to China (1944), and Padiham and District 'Salute the Soldier Week' (May 1944).

In addition to being the choreographer, Gladys was also the manager, bill-poster and seamstress for the troupe, who are seen here in outfits which were made before the outbreak of war. In this picture, taken in 1940, the members of the troupe are, from left to right: Teresa Wynne, -?-, -?-, Freda ?, Ethel Taylor, Marion Exton, Vida Rigg, Peggy Johnson, -?-, May Fothergill and Agnes Wynne. Tiny the Trickster, dressed in sash and skirt, was a favourite with audiences for his cute ways. His last appearance was on 17 March 1945.

Haslingden Squadron Air Training Corps on camp at HMS *Blackcap*, at Stretton, Warrington, August 1945. James Rishton is eighth from the right on the back row. He spent several years in the ATC before joining the RAF as a fitter. Amongst other things, the youths in the ATC went to various aerodromes, occasionally were given rides in aircraft and allowed to make simulated parachute jumps from landing-practice rigs. Another member of the squadron, Alan Edmonson, recalls:

As a boy, 13 years old when war was declared, I had much excitement, once the fighting started: Dunkirk, Singapore, Egypt, the pinholes in the map on the back of the pantry door showed the ebb and flow of the conflict. Air raid warnings meant an hour or two in the mill bottom of Hardman's Mill; then in the house cellar, then in bed, as the uniqueness of the event wore off. Later, in the top forms of Haslingden Grammar School, there was firewatching to do, taking a turn to sleep in the nicotine-smelling staffroom (male) until an air raid siren summoned one to duty and a chance to watch searchlights and the red glow on the southern horizon indicating that 'Manchester was getting it tonight.' Of course there were lighter moments – such as fire extinguisher fights on the top corridor – boys will be boys.

Bus travel was the order of the day as petrol was rationed, but Donald Heyworth used some of his to pick up boys from Rawtenstall for the Sunday morning parade of the Air Training Corps 1926 Squadron to which many Grammar School boys belonged, teacher Frank Barton being in charge. For some like myself it provided a good foundation for service in the RAF with summer camps at RAF Cranwell, and Cottishall, and a free flight in an RAF Anson from Squires Gate, Blackpool.

At eighteen I was called up and left the upper reaches of school – prefect, etc. and the dizzy height of Flt. Sgt. in the ATC, to become an AC2 in the RAF at Padgate. The old school uniform did come in handy as a disguise, allowing me to travel from Wiltshire back to Rawtenstall for a few days leave, beyond the distance of a normal 'pass'. Schoolboy one day, serviceman the next – such was the life, for me, in 1943.

Taken during Haslingden Youth Week, 1945, this photograph shows Sgt. Bill Sagar of the ATC demonstrating his hobby of model-making at the Handicraft Exhibition and Display, given at the Secondary Modern School.

During the war far fewer toys were manufactured, the factories having to concentrate on supplying goods vital to the war effort, as a result of which there was a growth in the number of home-made wooden toys such as loose-limbed acrobats, animals, delivery vans and aeroplanes. A toy railway engine could be made from something as simple as two rectangular tins and a round one, plus a flat piece of wood, eight tin lids and a few odds and ends.

Amongst the Girl Guides is the donor of the photograph, Mrs Rishton, née Webb. The boys are wearing the uniform of the Boys Brigade.

Schoolchildren from Lomeshaye, near Nelson, with the salvage they had collected for the War Effort, 19 September 1940. 'Waste not want not' could have been, and probably was, the slogan of many posters. Any scrap material had a value to the great struggle. One campaign was to persuade housewives to give up their old pots and pans to be turned into weapons.

One of the most noticeable long-lasting results on the environment brought about by salvage for the war effort was caused by the Emergency Powers (Defence) Act of 1940. Under this Act local and municipal boroughs were empowered to requisition all unnecessary iron or steel railings, posts, chains, bollards, gates, stiles, etc., and thousands of householders saw the ornate railings protecting their small gardens

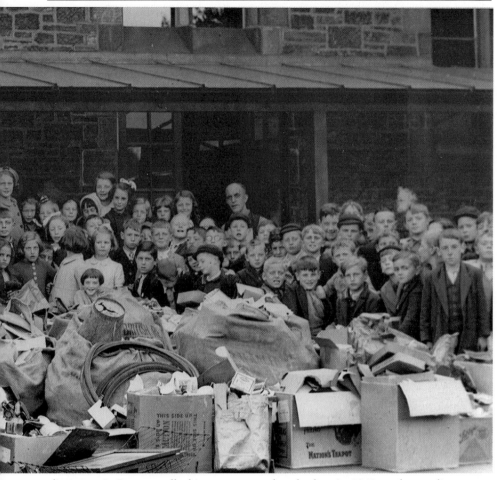

disappear. In Rawtenstall, this mass removal took place in 1942, and according to one old Rossendalian, 'the railings were taken to Leach's scrapyard where they stayed for the rest of the war'.

It is interesting that the letter announcing the removal of the railings included the following paragraph:

> It is hoped that owners will be prepared to make a free gift of their railings, etc., to the nation, but property owners and others whose interests are affected by the removal and who desire to claim compensation may obtain the appropriate form from the Town Clerk, Town Hall, Rawtenstall.

Close ties were forged between Rawtenstall and the members of the crew of HMS *Fancy*, funds for which were raised during the town's 'Warships' Week'. This photograph shows many children of the town enjoying a Christmas party arranged by the members of the crew, who had spent many of their leisure hours making a range of toys for Christmas gifts. The ship's badge hangs proudly in the library.

Section Eight

THE LONG-
AWAITED VICTORY

In 1995 the commemorations of the fiftieth anniversaries of VE day and VJ day followed different tones; the former was more of a celebration, whilst the latter was a more sombre affair, which took into account the dreadful and inhumane sufferings of the POWs held by the Japanese, and the dropping of atomic bombs on Hiroshima and Nagasaki.

In 1945 the two celebrations had more in common, for although the activities of VE day were spontaneous whilst the events for VJ day were organized, each was a festive occasion, as indicated by the Borough of Haslingden's official programme of celebrations for VJ and VJ-plus-1 days.

The list of events for VJ day commenced with an open air service of thanksgiving, followed by music and dancing from 1.30 p.m. to 9 p.m. in Victoria Park, a fancy dress procession at 1.30 p.m., at 7.30 p.m. the laying of a wreath on the cenotaph by Haslingden Youth Club, open-air dancing from 9.30 p.m. to midnight, and the lighting of a bonfire at 10 p.m. VJ-plus-1 day saw music and dancing from 1.30 p.m. to midnight, and on both days there were free pony and cart rides and donkey rides for the children, and free use of bowling greens, tennis courts, putting greens and public baths. No doubt similar celebrations took place throughout the country.

For some, though, the joy of victory could not compensate them for the loss of members of their families. Although East Lancashire had suffered little in the way of air raids in comparison with cities such as Manchester, Liverpool, Coventry or London, thousands of Lancashire people had gone into the armed forces, never to return. Of those who did come back, many were crippled or mentally disturbed, or both. Even now, over fifty years later, some old warriors find it difficult to discuss the events and situations in which they had found themselves. A single chance remark or a sudden thought can bring back a flood of recollections and a tear to the eye.

The world they came back to had changed. Churchill had been defeated in a General Election and the Labour Party had come into power promising the nationalization of a number of industries, a National Health Service, free education and a massive house-building programme. The country, however, had been brought to the brink of bankruptcy, and the hoped-for re-introduction of luxury goods had to be postponed. This was also the case for rationing, which continued in force in varying degrees until 1954.

The war had, however, been of a different kind than that previously experienced. With air raids likely to strike anywhere in the country, it had been the people's war; every man, woman and child had been a target. And yet, throughout it all, even in the darkest hours, there had been little talk of the possibility of defeat. The hills mentioned in Churchill's speech in the perilous days of 1940, when he declared '. . . we shall fight on the beaches, we shall fight on the landing grounds, we shall fight in the fields, and in the streets, we shall fight in the hills . . .' could well have been the Pennines of East Lancashire. A retreating army would have been supported by veterans of the First World War, backed by stern-faced Lancashire women and fresh-faced youths, and every square yard of land would have been costly to the enemy. One ex-bomb aimer and navigator recalled the day that war was declared. He and his friends were in Rhyddings Park, Oswaldtwistle, talking about what they would do if called up, using some strong language. A woman walking by overheard them, and called out, 'If you lads can fight as good as you can swear we've nothing to worry about'. Their time to fight did come, and it is probably right to think that if ever the time had come for that woman to fight, she too would have picked up a rifle. In the nineteenth century, after a long trade depression in which thousands of Lancastrian textile workers had endured great poverty, Lord Salisbury had stated, 'There is no finer thing on earth than a Lancashire man or a Lancashire woman'. The conditions of adversity might have changed, but the spirit was unaltered.

Northern Daily Telegraph

SPECIAL
PINK

59th Year.—No. 18129   TUESDAY, MAY 8, 1945   Price 1½d

Surrender To Be Ratified in Berlin

90 Seconds Handshake

Monty Greets Rokossovsky

**From DOON CAMPBELL,
Reuter's Special Correspondent**

WISMAR, Tuesday.
Field-Marshal Montgomery and Marshal Rokossovsky met here yesterday in a cobbled lane on the edge of the Baltic, in the little town where first contact was established between British and Soviet Armies.

A salute of 19 guns to Marshal Rokossovsky was fired as he inspected a guard of honour of "Red Devils" of the Sixth British Airborne Division. Red Flag and Union Jack flew side by side.

Then during a 90 seconds' handshake, Rokossovsky, beaming benignly, drowned Marshal Montgomery's first word with a flow of enthusiastic welcome.

"SHAKE AGAIN"

"It is a great honour to see personally and to greet a great soldier of this war," said the Soviet hero of Stalingrad and

PREMIER'S BROADCAST

United Nations Celebrate VE-Day

BROADCASTING TO THE NATION THIS AFTERNOON MR CHURCHILL SAID THAT THE GERMAN SURRENDER AGREEMENT WOULD BE RATIFIED AND CONFIRMED IN BERLIN.

An early meeting between Mr Churchill, President Truman, and Marshal Stalin is expected by United Nations diplomats at San Francisco.

They believe that only a gathering of the Big Three, probably in the European area, can solve some of the urgent problems arising from the defeat of Germany.

The final moves in the capitulation of Germany are being made. Prague, the Czech capital, is reported free again, while the British

—No 10 Damaged—

Premier Said "Carry On"

This story is told of the scene inside 10, Downing-street when it was damaged by a bomb.

Mr Churchill was having dinner at the time. The ceiling and chandelier came hurtling down, but the Premier was undisturbed. With characteristic coolness he remarked: "Carry on with the coffee."

Surrender of German Navy

No Trouble Expected

By Press Association Naval

NAZI PARTY DAYS OVER—Doenitz

Reuter

ADMIRAL DOENITZ TO-DAY ANNOUNCED THE END OF THE NAZI PARTY IN THESE WORDS:

"The foundations on which the German Reich was built are a thing of the past. The unity of State and party no longer exists. The Nazi Party has disappeared from the scene of its former activity."

Doenitz also stated that the "cease fire" in Europe would take place at 11 o'clock to-night. It is not known on what grounds the Allied Command has agreed to a delay of 42 hours after the reported signing of the surrender—it has done so—but it may be presumed that this period is necessary to get the order through to all German garrisons.

In a broadcast to the German and the Reich. Government formed by me, will be able to continue in office or not.

"When I addressed you on May 1 to announce the death of the Fuehrer and my appointment as his successor, I told you that my first task would be to spare the lives of German men and women.

"In conformity herewith I ordered the High Command on the night of May 4 to arrange

"If I can be of assistance to our Fatherland by continuing in office I shall do so. My love for Germany and my sense of duty keep me at my difficult post without regard to personal considerations.

"I shall not remain an hour longer than is compatible with the dignity which I owe to the Reich.

The *Northern Daily Telegraph* of 8 May reported how various towns in the area celebrated the news of the surrender:

Today's first duty for housewives was a round of food shops, and there were the usual fish queues. The lifting of a weather security ban now permits it to be said that many women stood in heavy rain as they waited for their supplies.

Apart from bonfire preparations and the display of flags and bunting, Blackburn showed no outward signs of the day's rejoicings, the only official observance being the thanksgiving services in the Cathedral. Among the decorations in many streets were Siegfried lines of underwear and draped lampposts in memory of Hitler.

There were no abnormal crowds in the centre of Burnley. Everybody was quietly happy, with pent-up feelings waiting to express themselves after the word 'Go!' from Mr Churchill this afternoon. Meanwhile the younger element seized upon the situation. An effigy of Adolf Hitler was carried by one group of youngsters who urged the public to subscribe to his cremation. After the Prime Minister's announcement hooters, buzzers and whistles of local works were sounded for about five minutes. The Town Hall clock was illuminated last night for the first time since September 1st, 1939.

This morning members of the Nelson branch of the British Legion walked in procession led by a military band to the Cenotaph at Victoria Park. There was no wreath-laying, but just a simple gesture of respect to those who served in this war.

In Clitheroe Market Place there is a dais where the flags of the United Nations are flying.

Singing and waving flags, children flocked to the centre of Darwen this morning. The municipal buildings are gay with flags of the Allies and Dominions. The feeling of the children was indicated by one wee girl who said, 'I shall have a Daddy now, like the other girls'.

Throughout the war patriotic entertainers had sung, danced and joked to keep up the spirit of the nation, either in person or via the radio. Probably the most popular Lancashire comedian and singer was George Formby, who is seen here signing the visitors' book in the Town Hall, Blackburn, at a civic reception given in his honour in February 1942.

VE day celebrations, Milton Avenue, Clitheroe.

Victory Celebrations, Nelson Street, Low Moor, Clitheroe.

Victory Parade in May 1945, passing the saluting dais at the entrance of Corporation Park, Blackburn.

VE day celebrations outside Burnley Town Hall.

Accrington and Church Thanksgiving Week, 13–20 October 1945. The Queen was Miss Doreen Ormerod. This was one of the many thanksgiving celebrations which took place throughout the country.

Draughtsman - Left forearm amputated   Dressmaker - Left forearm amputated

Surgical appliances-Both legs paralysed   Gardener - Right forearm amputated   Carpenter-Left leg amput

Shorthand Typist - Blind   Watch & Clock repairer - Man - right leg amputated. Woman - both hips dislocated

Leather Machinist - Left leg amputated   Telephone operator - Blind   General Electrical Repairs-left leg and foot   Radio Mechanic-of the bone') right leg   General Office Work - Both hands o

This leaflet acts as a reminder that many people in the services, as well as civilians, did not survive the war without injury. It states:

> In 1941 the Ministry of Labour and National Service had started, as an interim measure, a scheme for the training and resettlement of disabled persons. The scheme had two objectives:–
> a) to help those who had suffered recent disablement, whether through war service, in air raids or from other causes, to take up employment of a kind suited to their disability.
> From early on in the war efforts were made to train and resettle people who had been disabled.
> b) to help those whose disability was of an earlier date to prove their capacity for useful work and to play their part in the war effort.
>   This interim measure was superseded by the Disabled Persons (Employment) Act of 1944, which included Vocational Training and Industrial Rehabilitation.

Little time was lost in getting disabled people back to work, for a representative from the local office of the Ministry went to the hospital in his area to interview any person who had a disability, and who needed advice and help to find suitable employment.

Prefabricated houses were designed for accommodating returning servicemen and people bombed out of their homes. On 30 April 1944 the first of many thousands of prefabricated homes went on show in London. Covering 616 sq. ft, the prefab had two bedrooms and a living room, bathroom, lavatory and kitchen – a single unit comprising wash-basin, washing copper, cooking stove, sink, and draining boards and refrigerator. The kitchen table folded neatly away into the wall. Prefabs were supposed to be able to be erected in a few hours by a small number of workmen. A supposedly temporary structure, and designed to last ten years, this one, the last in Rossendale, is still occupied.

Victory bonfire, Seat Naze, Waterfoot.

Mrs Wilson, who lost two sons in the last few months of the war, laying a wreath at the War Memorial, Haslingden, 11 November 1945. The Mayor is Billy Coupe; second from left is Mr J. Souter, the Schools' Attendance Officer who was also the Mayor's Attendant; the bewigged gentleman is Haslingden Town Clerk, Mr Burton.

At the same location as the 'Wings for Victory' parade in 1943, the WAAF's contemporaries march to commemorate the fiftieth anniversary of VE day.

On the fiftieth anniversary of VE day, Mrs Wilson's sons, and others who died, are saluted by their old comrades-in-arms and their sons and daughters.

Acknowledgements

I would like to express my appreciation to the following individuals for the loan of photographs and the time they gave to record their recollections:

Mr K. Beetson • Mr J. Bolton • Mr and Mrs E. Collinge • Mrs S. Darwent
Mr and Mrs N. Driver • Mr T. Dugdale • Mr A. Edmondson
Mr E. Edmondson • Mrs P. Edwards • Mr and Mrs T. Fisher • Mr A. Foster
Mr and Mrs W. Foulds • Mr S. Green • Mr K. Heap • Mr W. Houston
Mr K. Hughes • Mr B. Joynson • Mrs S. McConville • Mr and Mrs E. Pollard
Mr and Mrs J. Rishton • Mr B. Scully • Mrs G. Small • Mrs M. Smithson
Mrs I. Stevenson • Mrs E. Tattersall • Mrs J. Tattersall • Mr J. Williams
Mr A. Walton • Mr Watson

My thanks are also due to the staff of the following museums and libraries for the use of photographs, newspapers and documents:

Bury Museum, Rossendale Museum, Towneley Hall Museum, Whitworth Museum, Accrington Library, Blackburn Library, Bury Library, Clitheroe Library, Nelson Library, Rawtenstall Library.

My thanks are also due to the Algerines Association and Rolls-Royce Ltd, the *Rossendale Free Press* and the *Burnley Express*.

Scunthorpe, *D Taylor*
Skegness, *W Kime*
Around Skegness, *W Kime*

LONDON

Balham and Tooting, *P Loobey*
Crystal Palace, Penge & Anerley, *M Scott*
Greenwich and Woolwich, *K Clark*
Hackney: A Second Selection, *D Mander*
Lewisham and Deptford, *J Coulter*
Lewisham and Deptford: A Second Selection, *J Coulter*
Streatham, *P Loobey*
Around Whetstone and North Finchley, *J Heathfield*
Woolwich, *B Evans*

MONMOUTHSHIRE

Chepstow and the River Wye, *A Rainsbury*
Monmouth and the River Wye, *Monmouth Museum*

NORFOLK

Great Yarmouth, *M Teun*
Norwich, *M Colman*
Wymondham and Attleborough, *P Yaxley*

NORTHAMPTONSHIRE

Around Stony Stratford, *A Lambert*

NOTTINGHAMSHIRE

Arnold and Bestwood, *M Spick*
Arnold and Bestwood: A Second Selection, *M Spick*
Changing Face of Nottingham, *G Oldfield*
Mansfield, *Old Mansfield Society*
Around Newark, *T Warner*
Nottingham: 1944–1974, *D Whitworth*
Sherwood Forest, *D Ottewell*
Victorian Nottingham, *M Payne*

OXFORDSHIRE

Around Abingdon, *P Horn*
Banburyshire, *M Barnett & S Gosling*
Burford, *A Jewell*
Around Didcot and the Hagbournes, *B Lingham*
Garsington, *M Gunther*
Around Henley-on-Thames, *S Ellis*
Oxford: The University, *J Rhodes*
Thame to Watlington, *N Hood*
Around Wallingford, *D Beasley*
Witney, *T Worley*
Around Witney, *C Mitchell*
Witney District, *T Worley*
Around Woodstock, *J Bond*

POWYS

Brecon, *Brecknock Museum*
Welshpool, *E Bredsdorff*

SHROPSHIRE

Shrewsbury, *D Trumper*
Whitchurch to Market Drayton, *M Morris*

SOMERSET

Bath, *J Hudson*
Bridgwater and the River Parrett, *R Fitzhugh*
Bristol, *D Moorcroft & N Campbell-Sharp*
Changing Face of Keynsham,
  B Lowe & M Whitehead

Chard and Ilminster, *G Gosling & F Huddy*
Crewkerne and the Ham Stone Villages,
  G Gosling & F Huddy
Around Keynsham and Saltford, *B Lowe & T Brown*
Midsomer Norton and Radstock, *C Howell*
Somerton, Ilchester and Langport, *G Gosling & F Huddy*
Taunton, *N Chipchase*
Around Taunton, *N Chipchase*
Wells, *C Howell*
Weston-Super-Mare, *S Poole*
Around Weston-Super-Mare, *S Poole*
West Somerset Villages, *K Houghton & L Thomas*

STAFFORDSHIRE

Aldridge, *J Farrow*
Bilston, *E Rees*
Black Country Transport: Aviation, *A Brew*
Around Burton upon Trent, *G Sowerby & R Farman*
Bushbury, *A Chatwin, M Mills & E Rees*
Around Cannock, *M Mills & S Belcher*
Around Leek, *R Poole*
Lichfield, *H Clayton & K Simmons*
Around Pattingham and Wombourne, *M Griffiths,*
  P Leigh & M Mills
Around Rugeley, *T Randall & J Anslow*
Smethwick, *J Maddison*
Stafford, *J Anslow & T Randall*
Around Stafford, *J Anslow & T Randall*
Stoke-on-Trent, *I Lawley*
Around Tamworth, *R Sulima*
Around Tettenhall and Codsall, *M Mills*
Tipton, Wednesbury and Darlaston, *R Pearson*
Walsall, *D Gilbert & M Lewis*
Wednesbury, *I Bott*
West Bromwich, *R Pearson*

SUFFOLK

Ipswich: A Second Selection, *D Kindred*
Around Ipswich, *D Kindred*
Around Mildenhall, *C Dring*
Southwold to Aldeburgh, *H Phelps*
Around Woodbridge, *H Phelps*

SURREY

Cheam and Belmont, *P Berry*
Croydon, *S Bligh*
Dorking and District, *K Harding*
Around Dorking, *A Jackson*
Around Epsom, *P Berry*
Farnham: A Second Selection, *J Parratt*
Around Haslemere and Hindhead, *T Winter & G Collyer*
Richmond, *Richmond Local History Society*
Sutton, *P Berry*

SUSSEX

Arundel and the Arun Valley, *J Godfrey*
Bishopstone and Seaford, *P Pople & P Berry*
Brighton and Hove, *J Middleton*
Brighton and Hove: A Second Selection, *J Middleton*
Around Crawley, *M Goldsmith*
Hastings, *P Haines*
Hastings: A Second Selection, *P Haines*
Around Haywards Heath, *J Middleton*
Around Heathfield, *A Gillet & B Russell*
Around Heathfield: A Second Selection,
  A Gillet & B Russell
High Weald, *B Harwood*
High Weald: A Second Selection, *B Harwood*
Horsham and District, *T Wales*

Lewes, *J Middleton*
RAF Tangmere, *A Saunders*
Around Rye, *A Dickinson*
Around Worthing, *S White*

WARWICKSHIRE

Along the Avon from Stratford to Tewkesbury, *J Jeremiah*
Bedworth, *J Burton*
Coventry, *D McGrory*
Around Coventry, *D McGrory*
Nuneaton, *S Clews & S Vaughan*
Around Royal Leamington Spa, *J Cameron*
Around Royal Leamington Spa: A Second Selection,
  J Cameron
Around Warwick, *R Booth*

WESTMORLAND

Eden Valley, *J Marsh*
Kendal, *M & P Duff*
South Westmorland Villages, *J Marsh*
Westmorland Lakes, *J Marsh*

WILTSHIRE

Around Amesbury, *P Daniels*
Chippenham and Lacock, *A Wilson & M Wilson*
Around Corsham and Box, *A Wilson & M Wilson*
Around Devizes, *D Buxton*
Around Highworth, *G Tanner*
Around Highworth and Faringdon, *G Tanner*
Around Malmesbury, *A Wilson*
Marlborough: A Second Selection, *P Colman*
Around Melksham,
  Melksham and District Historical Association
Nadder Valley, *R. Sawyer*
Salisbury, *P Saunders*
Salisbury: A Second Selection, *P Daniels*
Salisbury: A Third Selection, *P Daniels*
Around Salisbury, *P Daniels*
Swindon: A Third Selection, *The Swindon Society*
Swindon: A Fourth Selection, *The Swindon Society*
Trowbridge, *M Marshman*
Around Wilton, *P Daniels*
Around Wootton Bassett, Cricklade and Purton, *T Sharp*

WORCESTERSHIRE

Evesham to Bredon, *F Archer*
Around Malvern, *K Smith*
Around Pershore, *M Dowty*
Redditch and the Needle District, *R Saunders*
Redditch: A Second Selection, *R Saunders*
Around Tenbury Wells, *D Green*
Worcester, *M Dowty*
Around Worcester, *R Jones*
Worcester in a Day, *M Dowty*
Worcestershire at Work, *R Jones*

YORKSHIRE

Huddersfield: A Second Selection, *H Wheeler*
Huddersfield: A Third Selection, *H Wheeler*
Leeds Road and Rail, *R Vickers*
Pontefract, *R van Riel*
Scarborough, *D Coggins*
Scarborough's War Years, *R Percy*
Skipton and the Dales, *Friends of the Craven Museum*
Around Skipton-in-Craven, *Friends of the Craven Museum*
Yorkshire Wolds, *I & M Sumner*